To Frank all the Best

Allen Toussaint

The Last of the Four Musketeers

→ ←

ALLEN JOE'S LIFE AND FRIENDSHIP
WITH BRUCE LEE

Allen Joe
with Svetlana Kim and Dmitri Bobkov

BALBOA
PRESS

A DIVISION OF HAY HOUSE

Copyright © 2015 by Svetlana Kim and Dmitri Bobkov.

All rights reserved. No part of this book may be used or reproduced by any means, graphic, electronic, or mechanical, including photocopying, recording, taping or by any information storage retrieval system without the written permission of the author except in the case of brief quotations embodied in critical articles and reviews.

BRUCE LEE® and the Bruce Lee signature are registered trademarks of Bruce Lee Enterprises, LLC. The Bruce Lee name, image, likeness and all related indicia are intellectual property of Bruce Lee Enterprises, LLC. All Rights Reserved. www.brucelee.com

"Be Water" Quote: © Bruce Lee Enterprises, LLC. All Rights Reserved.

Balboa Press books may be ordered through booksellers or by contacting:

Balboa Press
A Division of Hay House
1663 Liberty Drive
Bloomington, IN 47403
www.balboapress.com
1 (877) 407-4847

Because of the dynamic nature of the Internet, any web addresses or links contained in this book may have changed since publication and may no longer be valid. The views expressed in this work are solely those of the author and do not necessarily reflect the views of the publisher, and the publisher hereby disclaims any responsibility for them.

The author of this book does not dispense medical advice or prescribe the use of any technique as a form of treatment for physical, emotional, or medical problems without the advice of a physician, either directly or indirectly. The intent of the author is only to offer information of a general nature to help you in your quest for emotional and spiritual well-being. In the event you use any of the information in this book for yourself, which is your constitutional right, the author and the publisher assume no responsibility for your actions.

Any people depicted in stock imagery provided by Thinkstock are models, and such images are being used for illustrative purposes only.
Certain stock imagery © Thinkstock.

Print information available on the last page.

ISBN: 978-1-5043-4296-4 (sc)
ISBN: 978-1-5043-4298-8 (hc)
ISBN: 978-1-5043-4297-1 (e)

Library of Congress Control Number: 2015916946

Balboa Press rev. date: 11/9/2015

Empty your mind, be formless, shapeless like water.
Now, if you put water in a cup, it becomes the cup.
You put it in a teapot and it becomes the teapot.
Now, water can flow or creep or drip or crash.
Be water, my friend.

— Bruce Lee

Contents

Foreword ix
Acknowledgments xiii
Prologue xv

Chapter 1　Childhood and Youth: Shaping of the Character .. 1
Chapter 2　War in the Pacific: My Jade Ring 12
Chapter 3　Back Home: Beginning of a New Journey 26
Chapter 4　Bodybuilding: Who Was the First 35
Chapter 5　Friendship: "All for One, One for All" 59

Epilogue 85
Appendix 87
Bibliography 89
About the Authors 91

Foreword
by Linda Lee Cadwell

MY UNCLE ALLEN

My Uncle Allen is an exceptional man. I am proud and grateful to call him my friend and mentor. In the 50-plus years I have known Allen Joe, he has taught me many things: the importance of family and friends; the value of loyalty; having the courage to stick to your beliefs; and having respect and love for those who have gone before.

When Bruce and I were married in 1964, we moved to Oakland and lived with James Lee, his wife, and two children. As you will read in the story of his life, Uncle Allen and James were long-time friends, and Allen had met Bruce recently in Seattle. Shortly after moving in with James, I was introduced to Allen and George Lee. James, Bruce, Allen, and George became the Four Musketeers. Martial arts drew them together initially, but their unique personalities formed a bond that lasted throughout their lifetimes and beyond. That bond was one of friendship and trust. It is important to know Allen's story because he is the last of the musketeers. Speaking from my perspective as Bruce's wife, I can tell you that as Bruce's popularity shot sky-high and he was being inundated by offers, it was the friendship of his closest friends, including the other three musketeers, that he treasured the most.

Even though I have known Uncle Allen and his beautiful wife, Auntie Annie, for so many years, in reading this book I learned many stories from his early life that I had not heard before. Thinking about his experiences in World War II, I reflect on the fact that without Allen and thousands of other soldiers, this nation may not have been a place where Bruce Lee could have thrived in a time of peace. Allen's experiences of overcoming racial prejudice were great lessons for Bruce. If Allen had not been a body building champion, perhaps Bruce would not have been motivated to take up weight training and improve his fitness overall. From Allen's example, Bruce saw a successful entrepreneur and a model father and husband. We have to remember that Bruce was only eighteen and had been in the United States only a few months when he met Allen. Having been born in San Francisco, but raised in Hong Kong from the age of three months, Bruce did not know much about the Western way of life. It was friends like James, George, and Allen who became role models for Bruce and enabled him to make his assimilation into American society easier.

I am gratified to call Allen and Annie Joe my friends over all these years, since we met in 1964. Many were the good times we had in those early years when our families were young. After Bruce left us, times were not always good, but Allen and Annie were always there for me. Steadfast in their concern for my welfare, they have never wavered in their support of my family. Allen's encouragement has inspired me to do my best to protect Bruce's legacy. His frequent calls and many boxes of See's chocolates have told me how much he has cared for my well-being and happiness. Bruce, too, would be thanking Allen and Annie for being my guardian angels.

I would like to thank Svetlana Kim and Dmitri Bobkov for taking the initiative to write this book. They realized the importance of Allen's life story for historical reasons and also as an example for those who feel they are facing insurmountable obstacles. The fact that Allen's compassion and kindness were influential in Bruce Lee's coming of age illustrates how any one of us may inspire a friend to reach for his or her potential.

Uncle Allen – you have had a long and fruitful life. I cannot say it better than Ralph Waldo Emerson:

> "The purpose of life is to be useful, to be honorable, to be compassionate, to have it make some difference that you have lived and lived well."

That is you, Uncle Allen Joe.

With respect and love,

Linda Lee Cadwell, President of Bruce Lee Foundation

Acknowledgments

My wife Annie remains the greatest blessing of my life for her love and daily reminders of what it is that truly matters. She knew the story I wanted to tell before I did. I'm sharing some of the most personal things about my life that I've never expressed publicly to anyone. Annie gave me the confidence to proceed.

To my children: Donna, Annette, and Darrell; thank you for your support with this story.

To my friend Tommy Gong, my life has been enriched getting to know you.

Svetlana Kim and Dmitri Bobkov, working with you has been a real gift. Hours of conversations served as a basis for the beginning of this book.

My gratitude to Quinn Dalton and Jamey Bradbury for editing my book with professional care. Their contributions are invisible to you, but I appreciate their superb efforts.

Special thanks to Linda Lee Cadwell and Shannon Lee for their enormous help with this project and, most of all, for their decades of friendship, and a deep thank you to everyone who has contributed to bring this book to you.

Prologue

The Four Musketeers

We were the Four Musketeers: James Lee, George Lee, Bruce Lee, and me, Allen Joe. I often think of them—my friends who have since passed away—and each of them appears alive and full of vigor in my memory again. I remember how each of us, unique and determined, bonded into a family, a shared universe of deepest truths and understanding. How our lives became inseparable from one another's. How we became the Four Musketeers. And how, like the original four musketeers, we lived by the motto "all for one, one for all."

The friendship we had, and the ways we looked out for one another, and the ways we learned from each other were priceless. I, Allen Joe, the last of the Four Musketeers, want to share that with you.

Along with James', George's, and my own story I want to tell you Bruce Lee's story — the story of improbable and yet undeniable success as a Chinese American celebrity, a leader and a thinker who accomplished so much and died too soon. This is the story of friendship and achieving excellence against all odds.

This book is our story. And, now, let me begin.

Chapter 1

Childhood and Youth: Shaping of the Character

> A man's character is his fate.
> — Heraclitus

"He hanged himself!"

I ran to the window and with one quick move pulled the shades. I had done it so many times that I didn't even need to think about it. The room became dark and filled with anticipation and uncertainty. My mom always made me pull the shades when something happened in our neighborhood and the town crier brought the latest horrifying news. Because of her fears of Tong, Chinese gang men, and not wanting to provoke them in any way, my mom would not permit us to look outside.

"He hanged himself because of an unpaid gambling debt! He chose to hang himself instead of waiting to be killed!" the town crier continued to scream. His voice was as striking as the sound of a church bell that echoed through the empty street and resonated inside my house.

My mom, younger brother, and I were quietly standing on a cold wooden floor far away from the windows, hiding, as if someone could still see us through the curtains. I felt a small stream of sweat from my temple run like a snake slowly down over my face under the collar of my shirt, making me shiver as it continued its way down my back. It seemed that time had stopped moving.

Footsteps of our neighbors broke the silence — we shared a house with two other families, as well as a small communal bathroom that had a large wash tub that we used as a bathtub, though it was hard to understand what it was made of. That was pretty much how everyone lived in our neighborhood.

Our neighborhood: Oakland, California, Chinatown of the 1920s and 1930s, with poor sanitation and habitations. It had well-organized tribunals of its own to punish offenders when it was in their interest to punish. Indeed, our neighborhood was very isolated with its complex society.

It was a time when arranged marriages were still in practice. In the early twentieth century, the advent of photography modernized traditional arranged marriages in Asia. Photographs and letters replaced face-to-face meetings between families and matchmakers. It became the "picture bride" system. For the first time, prospective couples living in different parts of the world could be introduced. Pressured to get married by his own father, my dad, who lived in California, decided to take advantage of that new technology, since there were not many options due to the very low number of Chinese females in America.[1]

---

[1] America's Chinatowns in the late nineteenth and early twentieth centuries were disproportionately populated by men. This happened due to the Chinese Exclusion Act that the U.S. Congress passed in 1882 and renewed in 1892. It was one of the most significant restrictions on free immigration in U.S. history, prohibiting all immigration of Chinese laborers. As a result, male laborers who came to the U.S. to work on the railroad could not be reunited with their families back in China. When the Act expired, Congress extended it a second time for another 10 years. This extension

That was how my mother, Florence, came here as a bride of U.S. citizen Henry Quong Joe.

My father had been a Navy man in World War I and served until he was honorably discharged. I was born in 1923. I hardly ever saw my dad; he ran a business back on the East Coast. Nevertheless, my little brother Kenneth was born six years later.

My father's relatives were all here on the West Coast. My dad's father was a very successful businessman. He owned several meat markets and jewelry businesses. I remember my mother playing mahjong with Chinese opera stars at our home. Life was good for a while, but those days ended when Dad left us.

I remember my father telling me goodbye. He paused for a moment as if he were trying not to forget to tell me something that was important. Then he said, "Take care of your mother." He was waiting for the streetcar. I had the feeling that I was seeing him for the last time. I was ten years old.

After that, we lost track of him. But that image of my father jumping on the streetcar and vanishing into the unknown, leaving me alone in the middle of the street, is still in front of my eyes now. The pain is always there. "Why did he desert me?" I wondered. (Years later, when I grew up, I tried to track him down, just to find out that he had died of leukemia at the age of seventy-five and was buried in a Navy cemetery in Florida).

Soon, my grandfather passed away. My mom was struggling to raise us — it was time for me to help my family.

So at the age of thirteen, I learned the meat cutting trade and became a butcher's apprentice. That was my first job; later, I worked as a newspaper boy, but not for long. At sixteen, I moved to Berkeley, where I was given room and board for working in a mom-and-pop

---

was made permanent by a Congressional action in 1902 and was the law of the land until Congress finally repealed it in 1943. For more information on Chinese Immigration and the Chinese Exclusion Acts visit http://history.state.gov/milestones/1866-1898/chinese-immigration.

grocery store in the meat department. It was then that I became interested in the gymnastic rings and horizontal bars at the James Kenny Park in Berkeley. The bodybuilding started later on, in 1939.

It started with me looking at *Health Magazine* where I saw a Charles Atlas ad. The ad showed a skinny guy named Mac getting sand thrown at him and saying, "Some bully bullied me!" I remember like it was yesterday: "The Insult that Made a Man Out of Mac!" It promised the seven-day "path to perfect manhood."

The more I looked at the ad, the more I believed its message. It was a story in the format of an American comic book. My attention was immediately drawn to the bully's muscular body, which implied a threat to the skinny Mac. The ad pulled me like a magnet and sucked me into it. All of sudden, I became Mac.

Then Mac's girlfriend Grace informed me of the bully's reputation. The huge bully had humiliated Mac by commenting on the smaller man's size; it became kind of personal to me.

Mac angrily takes matters into his own hands when he decides to order the magazine to start his exercises. I was ready to buy that magazine; with my free hand, I was going through the change in my pocket, not taking my eyes from the ad. The ad's vivid transition then showed Mac posed in a mirror to exhibit his new masculine body; then he returns to the beach, simply waves his fist, and the bully backs off. I was proud of Mac!

Wow, it looked so easy! My problem was solved! That's what I thought, running to the magazine stand to buy that magazine. Yes — it was right there, the solution to my problem — with the fastest health-, strength-, and physique-building system. Without hesitation I paid twenty-five cents. My heart was pumping hard as I scanned through the pages.

> The World's Most Perfectly Developed Man, Charles Atlas, born Angelo Siciliano in 1893, developed his body-building program on his own, inspired by the stretching of lions and tigers at

Brooklyn's Prospect Park Zoo. He began developing a series of isometric exercises that eventually gave him a classically sculpted musculature. He became "a new man" without the aid of weights or drugs. He was named "The World's Most Beautiful Man" and "The World's Most Perfectly Developed Man." His "Dynamic Tension" equipment-free body-building program used comic narratives to demonstrate its benefits, such as Mac's story — based in part on Atlas' own experiences.[2]

He was a hero and a role model to me because I had been bullied in school, and I didn't have a father to show me what to do. Because of him, I began to think about taking good care of myself, getting stronger, and getting good nutrition. I could have been a kid who got into trouble; instead, I worked to improve myself.

Dynamic Tension is a self-resistance exercise method which pits muscle against muscle. Practitioners would tense the muscles of a given body part and then move that body part against the tension as if a heavy weight were being lifted. It is nearly impossible to be injured during exercise using this method because your own muscles provide the force and, as they tire, the force used also decreases. Likewise, the benefits can continue beyond more traditional exercise methods because as you grow stronger, the exercise becomes more intense. I began to notice changes in my body soon, but of course not in seven days.

You might ask why anyone would want to work out without weights — especially since everyone now knows that using weights and machines is the fastest, most efficient way to gain size. Yes, this is true, but there are many reasons why someone might choose to train without the benefit of using weights.

---

[2] "Charles Atlas," *A&E Television Networks, LLC*, accessed March 16, 2014. http://www.biography.com/people/charles-atlas-9191659.

Someone working long hours may not have the time to get to a commercial gym, and may not have the extra space or money to set up a good home gym. Plus, in those days, most people thought lifting weights was pretty strange behavior. Coaches even warned athletes that weights would make them "muscle bound."

But I did not care; my muscles had grown bigger. Girls started noticing me, and guys looked cautiously at me. I wanted more muscles. Now, I had some money. So I started with a spring, and that was what I bought. That was my first exercise equipment. It was a big deal. Buying other equipment was expensive; therefore, I used empty cans, filling them up with cement and using them for weight lifting. Then I got some more money and I built my first weight set, eighty pounds. Oh, boy, I looked good in a mirror. My first gym was in a garage, which I rented for five dollars every month. That was how Ed Yarick and Jack LaLanne, two legendary pioneers of bodybuilding, both got started — in a garage.

In those days the only public gym was the YMCA, and it was mostly for swimming. It had very little equipment for power lifting, nothing for bodybuilding, and it was always crowded. That's the reason why Ed and Jack wanted to open a new kind of gym for bodybuilding. I met Ed Yarick through my best childhood buddy, James Lee. We had lived across the street from each other, had gone to the same school, and for some reason we always were interested in the same thing. I went to the gym; James was already there. Later on I started to take martial arts classes; James was also taking them but at a different location. If something bad or good happened to us, it happened almost at the same time.

Now, imagine the Ed Yarick Gym: Walking from the street you would see a tiny space, squeezed between other small storefronts on a busy block of Oakland's Foothill Boulevard, the dusty white blinds pulled down over the windows.

When you came inside, the first thing you'd see is a small wooden desk. We called it "Ed Yarick's office." This was where you paid your dues. It was an honor system; you simply put money in the upper drawer of his desk. Money was not important to him. He liked to train. Ed considered me a friend, and if you were his friend, he would never charge you a penny. He was that kind of man. After Ed marked you down as a member, he would walk you through the beginner's routine. And you were being given the very same treatment he gave to Steve Reeves, the "man's man," legendary bodybuilder, and Hollywood star. That was Ed Yarick.

You walked all the way to the back into a long, narrow room with a slant board for sit-ups and the leg extension apparatus. Next to it, a little further back, you could see metal shower stalls with plastic curtains and a tiny bathroom. There was a bench to sit on. You changed your clothes and put them in your bag by the wall — that was our "locker room." Through an open door next to the stall showers, you could glimpse a small backyard with benches, dumbbells, and barbells.

You turned around and went back, passing a lat pulldown, a cable row, a leg extension device, and a vertical leg press. Along one wall you'd see fixed-weight barbells that were racked vertically like the Pyramids of Giza. Against the other wall was an endless rack of dumbbells. Above the weights were mirrors and framed photographs of famous weight lifters looking down at you, watching your every move.

And finally, the center of the room. You'd carefully step onto a slightly elevated wooden platform which was reinforced with metal four-by-fours and lit from above by a skylight window. Two Olympic sets, lots of plates, a squat rack, and a heavy-duty flat bench would be waiting for you. Right there, next to you, a small box on the floor with chalk in it. You put chalk on your hands, firmly grip the Olympic bar, heart beating fast, and you'd feel the adrenaline rush as you lifted the weight. Yes! You did it!

That was my kind of gym — nothing fancy, simple and right to the point. The attraction of that gym was Ed Yarick. The man himself was the ambiance of that place. I remember that he liked soy nuts and always offered them to the kids. "Have you tried these?" he would ask with a big smile. "They are good and good for you." And they were really good.

I do not recall many women coming to his gym, but even so, everyone was welcomed there.

Ed Yarick was a big guy. He was six feet four inches tall and weighted more than two hundred and fifty pounds. If he had wanted to be intimidating, he could have been. But instead he was kind, good-natured, and friendly. He liked jokes. For a while he not only trained Steve Reeves but he was also his training partner. I happened to be training with them at that time. They were like two giants, tossing dumbbells, swinging barbells, making you wonder if they were real.

Through Ed Yarick I met Jack LaLanne, the "godfather of fitness." They were good friends and often performed handstand shows together. I went to Jack's — one of the nation's first gyms — in Oakland when it was opened. It was in 1936. Oh, boy, it was a dream gym: bright lights everywhere, fancy floor with plush carpet, elaborate equipment, multiple shower units, locker rooms for men and women. This fitness gym became a prototype for dozens of similar gyms using his name. He was a real businessman and, at his gym, people were dressed like businessmen, too. It was a different crowd — not my cup of tea, and so that was the reason why I came back to Ed Yarick's place.

Back then everything was competitive, very competitive. And I liked to train with somebody bigger to push me that much harder. Ed Yarick, who had become my mentor, said, "Hey, you can do it! You train with me." And he started training with me. Ed was not only my friend and mentor, he also was a father and an older brother, since I did not have either one. He motivated me, not only to train harder, to lift more weight — he made me believe in myself, and that no matter what I COULD DO IT! Ed was the world's greatest motivator.

Of course I had been going to school all this time. In my Oakland Chinatown, which ran from the waterfront up to

10th Street along the Webster neighborhood, I went to Lincoln Elementary School and in the afternoon, like all Chinese children, I also went to a Chinese school, which I did not like much because it was hard to read and write in Chinese. We had a dozen such schools there. As I remember myself, I was always doing something. School, work — time was flying by.

Then I entered the Oakland Technical School; there, I became interested in gymnastics and in Reserve Officers' Training Corps, or ROTC. I was good at the rings. But my favorite was rope climbing. I could climb hand-over-hand with my legs stiff, using only my hands.

It was during these high school days when I started dating my wife, Annie, the love of my life. Annie had five brothers, and that was probably why she always hung out with boys. Annie was fun, easy to talk to, always happy and full of energy, a person that you want to be around. Plus she was very good looking. Annie was like a magnet for boys in our neighborhood; they liked to gather at her porch.

Her father did not like that; I did not like that either. And pretty soon she didn't have any visitors. Annie asked me, "Do you know what happened to all the boys? I do not see them any more." Oh, boy, did I know… but I shrugged my shoulders and said, "I have no idea."

Annie's father owned a successful restaurant that served both American and Chinese food in Chinatown. They had a car and were considered to be rich. Annie always laughed if someone told her that. It was funny, how in those days if you had a car you were considered rich.

One day her father invited me for Thanksgiving dinner, and I knew that I had been accepted by the family. Years later Annie said, "You were at our house every day. My family practically adopted you; yes, Allen, we raised you up. Everybody liked you because of your personality. Well, I liked you too, Allen. You were a very nice boy and you were very persistent; that was what I liked about you."

World War II sneaked up on us during our senior ball. Our graduation was held during a blackout. And after that, life was completely different.

As an Asian, I was required to wear a pin that said "American Chinese" when I was in public, so that I would not be mistaken for Japanese. But I had already decided that I wanted to join the Air Force and volunteer for the war.

Not waiting to be drafted, my classmate and I went to the Army recruitment post in San Francisco to enlist in the Air Force to be pilots, but both of us failed the math test, since it was more for college students than high school graduates. And so we could not get in.

At that time, with men enlisting in the war effort, the work force had diminished. Filling a gross shortage of manpower, the women, both young and old, would punch in to work at the shipyards, factories, and munitions plants across America. We called them "Rosie the Riveter"[3] girls. Rosie the Riveter was the star of a government campaign aimed at recruiting female workers for the munitions industry. Based in small part on a real-life munitions worker, but primarily a fictitious character, the strong, bandana-clad Rosie became one of the most successful recruitment tools in American history and the most iconic image of working women in the World War II era.

During the war, women increased the workforce by 50 percent. They operated heavy-construction machinery, worked in lumber and steel mills, unloaded freight, became streetcar drivers, and much more. Racial barriers were broken as various minority members went to work. So, I applied for a job at the shipyards in Mare Island, Vallejo.

The Liberty Ships were assembled there in the astonishingly brief time. Henry Kaiser, the owner of the shipyards where I worked,

---

[3] "Rosie the Riveter," *The Pop History Dig, LLC*, accessed March 12, 2015. http://www.pophistorydig.com/topics/rosie-the-riveter-1941-1945/.

and his workers applied mass assembly line techniques to building those ships. To me, it looked very dramatic when huge cranes moved slowly on wide rail tracks carrying prefabricated sections of the ship. This production line technique, bringing pre-made parts together, moving them into place with huge cranes and having them welded together by "Rosies" (or "Wendy the Welders," as they were called in the shipyards) allowed unskilled laborers like myself to do repetitive jobs requiring relatively little training to accomplish. And it was a job that I could not have gotten only few weeks earlier.

I was assigned to a crew, a small team of workers, and did what my team leader asked me to do, mainly helping to bring or remove chains after the crane swung the components of the ship into place on a deck to be pulled into position by big pulleys. We were working on a cruiser, *Helena*, that was damaged in a bombing. I cannot recall what that cruiser looked like, since I worked night shifts and the only thing that I can remember are burner's torches and welder's arcs sparkling like fireflies in the dark, and unbelievable noise as dozens of men hitting steel wedges with four-pound hammers together with "chippers" cutting off temporary welds with pneumatic chisels at any given moment — steel hitting steel. I felt as if I was inside of a steel drum (in those days, no one used ear plugs), and it was bone-chilling on the deck of that ship.

Soon my team got another assignment, and I followed them to the Richmond shipyard. There, I decided to get some training and went to Oakland vocational school (the same school where Annie worked as secretary) to learn burner skills; it took only a few weeks, and with a certificate of graduation in my pocket, I soon started to work as a burner. It was easy: the ship-fitter scratched a thin line with a sharp metal pointer on the surface of steel. Then, with a hammer and steel punch, he pricked the steel along the scratched mark so that I, the burner, would be able to follow the punched marks when I sprayed the line with flame from the torch.

But that job was not for long; soon enough I was drafted into the war.

Chapter 2

War in the Pacific: My Jade Ring

> Courage is almost a contradiction in terms. It means a strong desire to live taking the form of readiness to die.
>
> — G.K. Chesterton

Looking at my old jade ring, I can slowly submerge back in time, into the jungle of the Pacific Island New Guinea, which was covered with tall palm trees and a high wall of green grass. Annie had given me the ring before I left.

"Every American soldier going to the war should have a jade ring to protect his life," Annie told me with a trembling voice, holding back tears. In her open palm was a striking ring, oval and domed in its shape, with a bright and slightly translucent apple-green jade set in a rich yellow gold. It was made in a traditional Chinese design — simple, yet sophisticated.

Annie's choice for the jade ring was not accidental. We Chinese believe that jade is endowed with magical powers of protection and healing, saving the wearer from disaster and bringing good luck. It was a statement of her love and devotion to me.

I wanted to tell her so much at that moment all of my feelings for her—I cannot even say it now. Instead, I looked in her eyes, and then, without either of us saying a single word, we jumped into a hug. That hug said everything for us, everything that could not be said in words.

* * *

New Guinea is the second largest island in the world. Allied operations there were essential both to the U.S. Navy's drive across the Central Pacific and to the U.S. Army's liberation of the Philippines from Japanese occupation during World War II.

For us infantry solders, it was also a battleground of disease, with Monsoon rains of eight or ten inches a day turning streams into impassable rivers.

Instead of roads, there were only native tracks — dirt trails tramped out over the centuries through the jungle's growth. Rain quickly dissolved those footpaths into calf-deep, glue-like mud. We carried our weapons and equipment, staggering along in temperatures that reached into the high nineties, with a humidity level to match. The jungle swallowed men and equipment within the blink of an eye. Tiny coastal settlements were infected with mosquito-borne tropical diseases such as malaria and dengue fever. The malaria and dengue threats were as great as the threat of Japanese soldiers waiting for us in the jungle. And I was one of the ones who fell ill with dengue fever.

I remember waking up in a big army tent with intravenous fluids dripping from a glass IV bottle into my arm. One drop slowly after another. The second lieutenant chaplain was writing a letter for me; he wrote slowly, one word at a time, like the drips in my IV bottle. I was dying of dengue. With my eyes wide open, I was staring at the half-empty IV bottle. Then I saw the glare from my ring. And right away, it seemed like something had lifted me up high and dropped me hard. Everything shook inside of me.

"I am sick, but I am getting better and I will see you soon." That was voice of the chaplain. He was reading aloud the letter that he'd written for me. A letter to my Annie.

I looked at my jade ring. It winked back at me, reflecting its warm green light, and for some reason I became so happy. I knew that everything would be all right. The saddest moment of my life had turned into the happiest. I thought, *I will live.* I believed every word the chaplain had read to me. I said to myself, "I am getting better and I will see you soon." Little did I know that my best friend, James Lee, would soon have to fight for his life against malaria on one of the islands in the Philippines!

Time passed by and I got well. But then one morning I woke up and looked at my ring in shock. My jade was gone. I had the ring itself but no jade stone in it. My life protector, my lucky charm, was gone. I could not think about anything else but my jade. I looked for it everywhere I could think of. I had to find it.

And, amazingly, I did find it. I could not believe my eyes. There it was in the cut grass, next to the shower stalls, shining in the rays of sun and greeting me with its green light as if it were saying, *I am here.* It had been a one in a million chance to find it in that jungle. And yet, it happened.

In my free time I continued with what I liked most — weight training. I improvised with car parts from the army's motor pool or wrecking yard. I took a gear and put on a plate, whatever I could find. Once I said to the guys in my unit, "You got any scrap metal, give it to me. And when I get deployed, it is going to stay here, with you." I couldn't take it with me, and I did not want to. My intent was to leave it for other soldiers so they would have something to do in their free time — a way to relax, escape from the routine of working, eating, and sleeping. I didn't think about the fact that by doing this, I was boosting my unit's morale. In any case, my makeshift gym didn't get past the all-seeing eyes of my commanders. Like the old saying goes, no good deed goes unpunished: I was promoted to corporal.

On the island, I was not just the only Chinese but the only Asian of any background in my unit. Some of my army buddies had not even seen a Chinese person before. And they also did not know much about bodybuilding. So I started training others. We joked, told stories — we had a good time, forgetting the war for a little while. It was my second favorite thing, after letters from home.

Letters from home. They were like a breath of fresh air. At least once a month, I would get a letter from Ed Yarick. He would write me about the guys that I'd trained with. All of them were in the service. He was creating a certain extended family by telling us about each other regularly; to me it was a reminder — you are not alone. We were all still together despite the fact that we were thousands of miles away from home. It felt good to stay in touch like that.

Thanks to Ed's letters, I would get news about my friend James. At the end of his letters, Ed always asked, "Do you keep up with your training?" He encouraged me to stay fit. He took it hard that he could not fight with us because of his medical condition. He had episodes of epilepsy; I had helped him once when he'd had a seizure in the gym. But I would still say this to him today: Through your letters Ed, you fought with us!

Then there were letters filled with love from my Annie. She wrote me every week about everything going on in her life, and so I had a sense of her presence in my everyday life. She wrote about changing her work schedule from morning to later in the day, which was the time we used to spend together. By working during that time, it would be much less difficult for her to deal with the fact that I was far away. I knew that she missed me. I knew I had to come back home alive just for her. I was a lucky guy to have that girl. She wrote me, and I wrote her back. But all of my letters had to go through military censorship, and sometimes they looked more or less like puzzles, since some words, even whole sentences, were literally cut out from letters. We both laughed about it; what else was left for us to do?

I would receive letters from Annie so often that the guys in my unit started calling them "letters from Mrs. Joe." A soldier from Australia who had worked as a jeweler before the war made a beautiful wedding ring from a silver coin with this inscription: *It's always you.*

"Now, you are a married man." He said and put the ring on my finger.

I have never removed that ring since.

After I got that ring, I felt like there was another me. I had a diary where I wrote everything that I saw and experienced in my daily life as a soldier. By that time, I had learned what I was not supposed to write down, yet I was still too emotionally attached to it to let it go. But then my commanding officer petitioned a request to transfer me from the Army Signal Corps to an Air Force Communication Unit as a teletype operator. He was worried that in the commotion of a battle, I could be mistaken for an enemy and killed by our own troops. I was the only Asian American soldier on the island. And who knew why I had been sent there in the first place? Perhaps nobody thought that a soldier named Allen Joe could be Asian.

Anyway, before the next breakfast time, I was on my way into the jungle with my diary hidden under my belt, walking fast, so I could be back for breakfast on time. I made my way deeper into the jungle, cutting everything that was before me, choosing the most impassable route. I stopped to catch my breath and looked around. It was dark as the night. I was surrounded by trees, lianas, and tall grass, all bound together into a continuous green wall. I had found my hiding place.

Using my machete as a shovel, I started digging a final resting place for my book. I felt as if I were writing its last page that day. I buried my thoughts and my experiences deep in the jungle to

The Last of the Four Musketeers

avoid even the slightest chance of a problem. I simply did not want to give Annie any more worries for me than she already had.

In New Guinea, for some reason I wanted to be a gunner for a B-25 bomber. I'd had that dream since Army boot camp and from those days of basic combat training in Atlantic City, New Jersey where I was sent to learn landing techniques and tactics of fighting on a shoreline before going back to St. Louis, Missouri, to teletype operator school.

I remember the foxhole with its fifty-caliber heavy machine gun on a mount, and a drill sergeant standing next to it with his legs wide like the mount of the gun. "If you can shoot thirty-caliber, you won't have any problems shooting the fifty-caliber used by the Air Force," he said, sounding convincing. "Get down in that foxhole and shoot," the sergeant ordered, and stepped behind me. The machine gun was almost as big as I was. I jumped into the vertical, bottle-shaped hole. Standing there with only my head and shoulders exposed, I looked around and with no delay, almost in one continuous motion, I loaded my belt with ammunition, pulled the bolt, slowly squeezed the trigger, and fired the gun. It jolted me as it fired. The empty shells flying everywhere made high-pitched metallic noises when they hit each other. At that moment, I imagined myself on a plane shooting enemy aircraft; I kind of liked it.

But then I changed my mind when I saw a B-25 bomber landing with as many as a thousand bullet holes over the whole body of the plane. Only one crewman had survived. It was a frightening experience.

Soon I was transferred to the Philippines. The Japanese had held the Philippines since May 1942, when the awful defeat of American forces led to General MacArthur's withdrawal. But MacArthur was back, as he'd promised, to recapture Luzon, the biggest and most important island of the Philippines. This required a "softening up" of the enemy.

The amphibious landing of the American forces at Leyte Island had begun with the goal of destroying the Japanese fleet in its gulf. Of course, the Japanese had anticipated the American landing and had assembled the largest ocean task force ever assembled during the war. The Battle of Leyte Gulf had begun.

On Leyte Island, our troops took on the Japanese garrison. But even after we had taken control of the island, Japanese soldiers who had been hidden away continued to emerge and fight on, preferring death rather than surrender. We were on the doorstep of Japan.

There, in the Philippines, the war became too long for me. I couldn't wait anymore. I was in love and I wanted to propose, but in the proper way with an engagement ring. But how? I was in a war. Still, that did not stop me. I decided that I would surprise my love with a proxy engagement. As a proxy, I decided to ask my mother: a woman I loved and who loved me, who could ask another woman I loved to marry me. I knew Annie would remember that special day in her life. Like nothing else, I wanted her be happy! I wanted her to have the best, and I was ready to do anything for that. I was so sure that no one would propose like my mother could — I did not have any doubts.

All this time, when I was in the army, I sent my soldier's pay home (money was useless to me; I did not smoke or drink, and anyway, there were not many stores in the jungle to buy anything in the first place). My mother could not write or read English, and I could not write or read Chinese. So, all this time Annie was our only source of communication. But to my luck, in the Philippines, I met an Army cook who was able to write a letter in Chinese for me. In that letter, I asked mom to take my money and buy an engagement ring for Annie.

But mom had a different plan.

Mom took her own savings and my money, called Annie, and suggested, "Let's meet today." Then she announced, "We're going to choose an engagement ring for you."

Annie told me later, "I did not know what to say, or how to react. I felt happiness and shock of surprise mixed all together. I was speechless, which is unusual for me. I walked quietly next to my future mother-in-law, trying to find the right words to express my gratitude for what she was doing for us. In a little while, I saw our destination, a jewelry store. I wondered how she would pay for the ring. I wondered this because your mother did not have a purse. But my thoughts were interrupted as soon as we entered the store. I forgot about everything — I felt blinded by the display of hundreds of sparkling diamonds; my head was spinning.

"Choose,' she said quietly to me. I said, 'This. I like this,' pointing to a small diamond ring. I wasn't even sure if I actually liked it, but there was too much to choose from."

"'No, it looks too cheap.' Your mother shook her head."

"'That one,' I said. My eyes became as big as the diamond stone of the next ring that I looked at."

"'No', she said again. She knew already what to buy. No matter what I chose, she would buy what she liked anyway. Plus, her father-in-law had owned a jewelry store, and she knew more about diamonds than me."

"'This one,' she said with a warm smile."

"Wow! I had not seen anything more beautiful than that ring. It was a ring that any girl would dream of. It was perfect to suit both my dress and my lifestyle. It was a platinum ring with a solitary diamond. It sparkled brilliantly.

"Your mother had an expression on her face, as if she bought engagement rings every day. She put her hand in a hidden pocket of her self-made Cheongsam, a body-hugging one-piece Chinese dress, (I never saw her wearing any European dresses), and pulled out a roll of money to pay for it.

"*That's where the money was,* I thought.

"At that moment, more than anything else, I wanted to show that ring to you, the ring that you gave to me. And as soon as I came home, I started to look for newspaper ads with images of rings that looked like mine and found one. I carefully cut it out and mailed it to you. Then you made a drawing of the ring from that newspaper clipping and mailed it back to me. I was surprised; it looked exactly like my ring. How did you do it?"

Annie still has that picture.

I was making plans for the future but the war was not over yet. Before I knew it, I was sent to Okinawa, but to catch my connecting flight I had to stop first at Palau, which had been liberated not long before. Palau, with its volcanic island, Peleliu — just six miles long and two miles wide — was held by a garrison of more than 10,000 Japanese troops. The island's airfield would allow Japanese planes to threaten any Allied operation in the Philippines; General MacArthur pushed for an amphibious attack to neutralize this threat. On the island there were many caves that were connected by networks of tunnels that allowed the Japanese to hunker down and emerge mostly unscathed from our bombardment. They held out for four days before we were even able to secure the southwest area of Peleliu, including a key airstrip.

I walked slowly, looking at the white clouds that were touching the top of the beautiful Umurbrogol Mountain, which the Marines had nicknamed "Bloody Nose Ridge." It was there that the advancing Marines had been blasted with heavy artillery fire and small arms bullets that pelted them like a heavy rain pouring from the network of rocky caves and tunnels. Someone told me, "It felt like every inch of that island was spitting bullets at you from all directions." Indeed, the Japanese used the island's unique terrain to their full advantage, stationing their soldiers in caves with only one goal — to kill the maximum number of our troops below.

Over the eight days of fighting, our armed forces sustained about fifty percent casualties. It was the most vicious and costly fighting of the Pacific campaign.

I stayed overnight in Palau, waiting for the plane to Okinawa. When I reported to the colonel in Palau, he told me, "We have a Chinese pilot who is from Oakland, too."

In my mind I was trying to imagine who it could be. I was eager to see him.

"That is his tent," the colonel said, showing me with a nod of his head the second tent from where we were standing. "You can wait for him right there," he said, and nodded again, this time toward a bench next to the tent. "He's coming from his mission now."

I sat and waited. It did not take long. Soon, I saw a Chinese officer walking to that second tent.

"Wait a minute," I thought, my heart pounding. I recognized him at the same moment he recognized me.

"William!" I yelled, jumping from the bench.

"Allen!" he yelled back, running toward me. We hugged each other. He was the second Chinese I had met since I'd entered the service and left Oakland. William was my buddy from the Oakland Technical High School ROTC program. Now he was a pilot, an Air Force officer. What were the chances that I would meet him over there?

William immediately invited me into the officers' tent for a meal. We ate and talked about our friends, about home. Before I left, William showed me some pictures that he'd gotten from home. We were so happy to meet, it felt as if we were home and there was no war. I guess to fully understand this feeling, one would have to be far away from family, friends, and home for a long time.

Next morning, I was on my way to Okinawa. From my days there, I remember a loud voice saying, "You're not going with the first wave of attackers." It was the voice of my commander. "The marines will shoot anything that looks Asian. You'll go with the second wave."

Okinawa was the last and largest of the Pacific Island battles of World War II. The Japanese changed their typical tactics of resisting at the water's edge to a defense in depth, designed to gain time. In conjunction with this, the Japanese Navy and Air Force mounted mass air attacks by planes on one-way suicide missions; they sent their last big battleship on a similar mission.

The "special attack" kamikaze tactics were so determined that we were really facing the most difficult phase of the war. A series of defense lines across the island enabled the Japanese to conduct a fierce defense of Okinawa over many weeks. Using pillboxes and strongpoints, caves, and even some ancient castles, their defense positions tightly supported one another and could resist even the most determined artillery fire and air strikes. Caves and pillboxes had to be destroyed individually with dynamite charges. Okinawa was a massacre.

I was standing on the snow-white sand beaches of Okinawa, trying not to think about what had just happened there over the last few weeks. The sand was so fine that I felt as if I were walking on cotton balls.

Okinawa was ours and we were preparing to invade the main island of Japan.

By the time I had become part of the Air Force, I was sure the war was going to end soon. But the Japanese forces had only stepped up their efforts to defeat the Allies, proving that they were even more deadly when faced with defeat. By late July, Japan was still refusing to surrender. There were estimates that invading Japan could cost another million American lives. This was why it was decided to use the atomic bomb.

Hiroshima was first, on August 6, 1945; three days later, Nagasaki was hit. At least 120,000 people died instantly in those attacks; tens of thousands more died from radiation exposure.

After that, I saw two white and green Japanese planes flying over Okinawa. I knew what that meant: Surrender.

For the Japanese in the Second World War, their national marking — a simple red circle known as the Hinomaru — was a powerful, elegant symbol of bravery, pride, and dominance. It was a symbol of Japanese aviators' nearly pathological pride in themselves, their service, and Japan. With the onslaught of kamikaze attacks, suicidal charges, and mass Masada-style suicides, the Americans had no trust in the Japanese peace envoys that might just as likely immolate themselves as actually surrender.

I had been told that as proof of peaceful intentions, the aircraft carrying the envoys from Japan to Lejima, the small Okinawa Island designated as the negotiation place, had to be painted white all over, and the beloved, honored, ancient Hinomaru had to be painted over in white and then replaced by the Christian cross — a green Christian cross symbolizing victory of life over death.

Frozen still, I continued to look at the two airplanes, which were painted all white, bearing on the sides of their fuselage and the top and bottom of each wing green crosses, as they flew over me, descending on the island. When I looked up at those two planes my heart almost jumped from my chest. Was this it? Was it all over?

I had witnessed history — the flight of those two planes became known as the Green Cross flights, envoys that signaled the unconditional surrender of the Japanese Empire.

In my memory I always block out the combat scenes and horror of the war and only think of episodes like that from time to time.

In the Air Force, my fellow airmen and officers had discovered my talent for drawing pin-up girls. They had seen my hand-drawn cards for Annie and the drawings on the envelopes in which I mailed her letters. So I was asked to draw pictures of "Petty's Girls" for my fellow airmen on the envelopes containing the letters they sent home. Each squadron had its own painting of "Petty Girls" on the front fuselages of their assigned bombers. I would copy that exact image on the envelope. My drawing on the envelope made it more personal; it was like a business card for them.

The "Petty Girl" was not just art for the fancy of men; she was a symbol for homesick GIs at war and was also a metaphor for the innocence of the times. She evoked memories of home and peacetime life and was a kind of psychological protection against the stresses of war and the high probability of death. The "Petty Girl" captured the classic pin-up look that has, in my opinion, never been matched since, and it's all due to one talented artist, George Petty.

Nose Art became one of the most recognizable forms of his work. It was not done by Petty himself but was actually copied from his work by other civilian artists or the occasional talented servicemen.

During the height of World War II, Nose Art artists were in high demand in every Army Air Force squadron. They boosted crew morale. Nose Art found its way onto bombers, fighters, cargo aircraft, and everything in between. I enjoyed doing it.

Serving in the Fifth Air Force Headquarters Squadron was different than fighting in the jungle; for that, I was ever so grateful to my commanding officer from New Guinea. He probably saved my life.

In Japan, I saw the famous Mount Fuji, and I visited Tokyo to find a place to learn judo. I had been introduced to it in boot camp and had been made an assistant to an instructor for my quick learning skills. I tried to learn, but it was difficult due to the language barrier. And all the while I was becoming more and more homesick. I wanted so much to go home.

After the victory, the War Department announced a point system for the demobilization and discharge of enlisted personnel. The point system had the objective of achieving equity in the demobilization. Soldiers were given one point for each month of military service and one additional point for each month of overseas service. Each battle star or decoration earned five points.

Soldiers were awarded twelve points if they had a child, credited up to a maximum of three children. A total of eighty-five points was needed for eligibility. If you had earned that number of points, you were to be demobilized as soon as transportation back to the United States was available. At that time I had sixty-nine points. I could not wait for my turn to be discharged.

I wanted to go home.

Chapter 3

Back Home: Beginning of a New Journey

> The seeker embarks on a journey to find what he wants and discovers, along the way, what he needs.
> — Wally Lamb

Home. Everything was welcoming: People were happy to see us, waving at us, greeting us with music. We could see that they were thankful for what we did. We were all heroes who'd fought for them and saved the country. We were Victory Soldiers. Posters with images of soldiers back home with their loved ones, driving new cars, moving to new homes as part of the American Dream, were all over ports and railroad stations on my way home; that kind of atmosphere made me feel proud for what I had done in the war. I was in a state of euphoria.

The one-hour car ride from the Sacramento airport was pleasant and no hardship compared to the voyage that I had just completed across the Pacific on a small cargo ship from Japan to Seattle. Those small cargo ships were called "Victory Ships."

Hundreds of them were used by the War Shipping Administration as part of "Operation Magic Carpet" to bring home over eight million American soldiers from the war.

I was trying to imagine Annie, her reaction when she saw me, what she would tell me first, what kind of dress she would wear — all that and many other things were going through my mind the last hour before we met.

Annie was very anxious to see me, too. She told me, "I wore a beautiful black hat that had cost me a fortune. I bought it after you sent me the message from Japan that you were coming home. For some reason, I wanted you to see me in that hat.

"I was all 'pins and needles,' sitting on the blue sofa in my best dress, facing an open window in our living room so I could hear and see everything that was happening outside. It was a warm sunny day, typical California fall weather. I could feel a light wind touching my face when I came close to the window. The street was practically deserted. My heart started beating fast with every car that passed by. I was afraid to miss you when you arrived. You had called to let me know that you were coming here in an hour. I looked at the clock on the mantle of our fireplace — more than an hour had passed since your call; I was counting minutes, jumping from the sofa every time I heard some noise outside. I could not wait another minute.

"You had never been in my new house. My family had moved into it while you were at war. I was afraid that you would get lost. All of a sudden, the noise of a stopping car and a closing door pulled me from my thoughts; I leaned over the window sill and saw that it was you, Allen. The light color of your uniform made the tropical tan of your face more pronounced. On one shoulder you carried your Army-issued drab green duffle bag that was faded from time, and on the other shoulder you had a big rifle, a war trophy for your kid brother. You looked like a guy from an Army poster — even better. I was ready to jump through the window. In no time I pushed the front door wide and shot outside. You saw me, too, and we raced to meet each other. You hugged me so hard that my hat flew away. We were together."

The war had confronted us all with numerous challenges. The government had found it necessary to ration food, gas, and even clothing during that time. We were asked to conserve everything. With not a single person unaffected by the war, rationing meant sacrifices for all. No one had complained. It was patriotic to conserve. The whole country had united in the face of adversity. People were helping each other without waiting to get anything in return; it was the norm of life.

Rationing was introduced to avoid shortages and to not allow only the wealthy to purchase commodities. But rationing made acquiring anything very difficult, and this continued after the war. Many people kept chickens both during and after the war and some even kept goats. Growing vegetables at private residences and in public parks in "Victory Gardens" helped with food supplies.

I remember after the war taking the ration books and going up to a store and getting my weekly ration of food. They would take a stamp out of the book and then it would be passed on.

"Red Stamp" rationing covered all meats, butter, and oils, and I believe cheese, too. Each person was allowed a certain amount of weekly points with expiration dates. "Blue Stamp" rationing covered canned and frozen fruits, bottled beverages, and vegetables, plus juices and dry beans, and processed foods such as soups, baby food, and ketchup. Ration stamps became a kind of currency, with each family issued a ration book. Each stamp authorized a purchase of rationed goods in the quantity and time designated.

In addition to food, rationing affected clothing, shoes, coffee, gasoline, tires, and fuel oil. With each coupon book came specifications and deadlines. Rationing locations were posted in public view. Rationing of gas and tires strongly depended on the distance to one's job. If one was fortunate enough to own an automobile and made sure to drive at the specified speed of thirty-five miles per hour, one might have a small amount of gas remaining at the end of the month to visit nearby relatives. Fine clothing was a real problem, especially for the young people who wanted to look fashionable for special occasions like weddings.

My mother wanted us to get married in January before the Chinese New Year. Traditionally, it is a very unusual thing to get married during the Chinese New Year in China, as it is the most important festival for the family and many people would not have time for a wedding.

At that time, my mother was living with my younger brother in a studio above the Yuen Hop Noodle Company and Asian Food Products shop that I used to work for before the war. That shop is the only place left on 824 Webster Street, in Oakland Chinatown, that is still owned by the original family. Even now, I am in contact with the owner's children who operate that store today. I am forever grateful to their parents, who gave me and my family a job and place to stay back then.

Mom gave me some money and a choice of having a house or a big wedding. I chose a house and rushed to find a place for Annie and me. Fortunately, after the war the government decided that something must be done to help World War II veterans like me assimilate into civilian life. Before the war, college and homeownership were, for the most part, unreachable dreams for most Asian Americans. But the GI bill provided a range of benefits for returning World War II GIs. Benefits included low-cost mortgages, low-interest loans to start businesses, cash payments of tuition and living expenses to attend university, high school or vocational education, and one year of unemployment compensation. Thanks to the GI bill, I could buy a house with low interest and zero down payment and live the American dream. But finding that house was not very easy. I was Chinese and I could not buy homes in certain areas. I did not want to stay in my old neighborhood and raise my family in America's Chinatowns.

In the broadest strokes, Chinatowns were products of extreme forms of racial segregation resulting from a web of laws, social practices, and ideas designed to shut out Asians completely from American life.

That was really how Chinatowns came into being. (Today, we think of them as a fun place to get a Chinese meal, but not as a way to contain a certain population and keep it separate from American life). Several Western states still had laws that prohibited Chinese from owning property. It was difficult to find white homeowners who would sell a home to us.

To my surprise, we found a home in Berkeley. And everything happened quickly. No real estate companies were in place at that time, and everything was by word of mouth. The seller was Chinese, our former high school classmate who was going through a divorce and needed to sell her house fast. It was a nice two-bedroom house. I bought it without thinking twice.

We got married on January 24, 1946, in a small church a few blocks from Annie's home, in Oakland. The first time I had ever been in a church was before my deployment in the war. It was a beautiful Catholic Church in St. Louis, Missouri. My Army buddy, a very religious Irish man, had brought me there.

The church was beautiful. Multicolored stained glass windows, the crucifix, icons with statues honoring religious figures, and hundreds of lighted candles. I did not know what to do. My friend explained that everything there had its symbolic meaning. The roof symbolizes charity, which covers a multitude of sins; the floor symbolizes the foundation of faith and the humility of the poor. I just looked around and listened to him, slowly moving to the altar, the center of the church. There, I was splashed with water, and we lit candles. It was the night after I had realized what might happen to me in the war. I was not scared; instead, I experienced a kind of inner peace. I thought about what was important to me.

The second time I was in a church was for my wedding. Annie wore a dressy suit, and I had a suit that I had worn at my high school graduation. It was a small ceremony, in a small house-like church just around the corner from the place where we lived. We did not have much money to spend on it, but it was an affair to remember! A wedding is normally considered a time of grand celebration, expenses, and people. We thought that our bonding, rituals, and feelings were going to be the same with or without countless people.

Annie said, "I remember you saying 'I love you.' I could see that you had some tears in your eyes and I almost lost it before the ceremony even began. I managed to pull it together, though. Just being up there with you, Allen, and saying our vows with only my older brother and my sister right there along with us was special."

Then it was the giving and receiving of rings, which is the most important part of a marriage ceremony. The preacher said, "These rings are made in the symbol of that which is eternal. There is no beginning and no end, and as you place these symbols on each other's finger, it signifies that there shall be no end to your marriage, and no end to the happiness that you will both share together."

At that moment I knew that I could not live without Annie. She was the one and only one for me. The preacher continued, "When people look at you, they will look at your hand and notice the ring on your finger. They will know that you belong to someone special, and that someone special belongs to you. So when you place these rings upon each other's fingers, wear them with love and with honor."

I gently placed the ring on Annie's finger; she placed the ring on mine. The preacher said, "Now, I pronounce you man and wife. You can kiss each other." I was the happiest man on earth that day.

Our marriage was an expression of joy, respect, dignity, and love. I always loved her, and the only thing that had stopped me from marrying her before was that I did not want to make her a young widow should I not come back from the war.

After the wedding, we all went to a local restaurant *Trader Vic* to celebrate. The next day Annie and I were on a train to L.A. for our honeymoon.

And who did I meet on that same train? It was my friend Ed Yarick going with his guys and my kid brother to Muscle Beach for a competition. Right away, he treated us to breakfast on that train. It was joyful to spend time with him after all those years.

At the train station, my army friend Dempster Dirk was waiting for us. He was a successful businessman of Dutch descent. Dempster had called me a week before we left and asked if I needed help finding a nice, inexpensive hotel not far from the beach. I was new to L.A., but he lived there and could get a good deal for me.

Dempster said, "I am not only going find you a hotel, I will also meet you at the station to drive you there myself."

And he did. A silver tray was his wedding gift, and it was waiting for us on the bed in the hotel room that he'd reserved for us. Something made of silver, according to the American wedding tradition, represents wealth and prosperity, and that was his wish for us.

He was my Army buddy, doing his best for Annie and me. We had met in Okinawa where he'd served as a Japanese translator; there, we'd became friends.

The next morning, in his new Chevy Coupe, Dempster drove Annie and me to show us the Exploratorium, a science center in L.A. Then he bought us a romantic dinner in a restaurant. We had the most private dining experience. Our meal began with a glass of French champagne and continued with a multiple course dinner. We were surrounded by luxury. It was an unforgettable evening and an unforgettable trip.

In L.A. we also went to the so-called birthplace of physical fitness, Muscle Beach, in Santa Monica, California — a stone's throw from Venice Beach, a short drive to Malibu. That site was known as a place where gymnasts, stunt people, acrobats, wrestlers, and weightlifters could all be seen on any given weekend. No beach in the nation, nor any other place on the planet, was as distinctly associated with the best bodies and athletes around. No other beach became the biggest destination for talented athletes as the one and only "Muscle Beach" of Santa Monica.

I just had to show that place to Annie. And it was there that I decided I wanted to compete in a bodybuilding championship.

We also visited Annie's favorite aunt Ruby. At her home, I tried freshly squeezed orange juice for the first time in my life. I still have that image in front of my eyes — a tall glass of orange juice packed with vitamins, radiating with sunshine freshness. I could see its exceptional color and sense its fruity aroma — it was alive. That was not the taste of orange juice that I was used to. The canned stuff was what most people knew as orange juice. In lieu of pricey fresh-squeezed juice, most Americans bought what the latest preservation technology offered: canned juice, which was essentially boiled to death. Unsurprisingly, its flavor was, let me say, somewhat lacking.

The rest of the time Annie and I spent on the beach lying in the sand, enjoying sunshine, blue, warm water, and every moment being together. It was a real honeymoon.

When we returned from that trip, we had a small family banquet to celebrate our marriage. We had the opportunity to enjoy all of our guests because we were a small group. I think otherwise it could be very difficult with a larger wedding to even have a chance to speak to everyone who attended.

Annie was stunning. She wore a beautiful Chinese dress with golden Phoenix birds symbolizing new life. It was amazing!

Let me mention that sixty years later, our children decided to make us a gift. Since we had not had a formal wedding before, they flew us to Hawaii. There, Annie and I renewed our vows standing on the golden sands of Waikiki in a traditional Hawaiian wedding ceremony, surrounded by our children and their families.

It felt as if I was young again. I felt exactly the same way as I'd felt on the day of our marriage; I was still madly in love.

Back then, in 1946, I wanted to become an artist. And I had even studied commercial art at the Gene Turner Art School in San Francisco for almost a year, but it was expensive. I tried to keep up with my payments by working as a model at that school, but it was still not enough. I had to support my family; that was my priority.

Using my mom's advice, I looked for a butcher shop to buy since it was my area of expertise at that time from my training in my younger years. A friend of a friend was selling his meat specialty store and opening a hot dog factory. I talked to him and got his store on East 14th Street, a few miles from my old neighborhood, Oakland Chinatown. I put a new sign above the entrance door. It said in big black letters, "Allen's Market," and with that I became a business owner.

It was not by accident that I decided to be a business owner; Chinese were still barred from most industries, aside from the hand-laundry and restaurant businesses. It was difficult for Chinese to find a place to live or work outside of Chinatown. White Americans basically did not want to work with the Chinese, and so Chinese people had to find work through self-employment. It was a struggle for Asian Americans living in America, but that kind of struggle can forge a person's character.

And that struggle gave birth to people like Bruce Lee, who was about to make the world a better place for all of us today. To be honest, at that time, I already knew that people could be very different and you never quite knew what to expect. Some of the kindest people I had met were white, and some Asian people would discriminate more against Asians than whites. I had already realized that change had to begin with the man in the mirror.

Chapter 4

Bodybuilding: Who Was the First

Anything in life is possible and you can make it happen.

— Jack LaLanne

"Who was the first bodybuilder?" I asked my friend, Jack LaLanne.

"It is not an easy question," he said. "But the answer to that question is, who is the first Asian to win a championship in bodybuilding in America? That's easy. It's you, Allen," Jack said, and then he laughed.

He was right. I was the first Chinese to win. It was 1946, and Jack LaLanne had been one of the judges.

It was the first interracial competition, and it had been judged with no discrimination. Competitors were represented by three races: Caucasians, African Americans, and Asians.

I remember how Ed Yarik talked me into it. "Allen, I know you can do it." And before I gave him my answer, he had signed me up. I knew that I did not have enough time to get ready for that competition but decided to do it anyway. I was just in that competitive mood, thanks to my friend, Ed.

The heavyweight and middle-weight divisions had five guys each, but light-weight had only three, including me. Back then, there were not many bodybuilders until Jack LaLanne built his chain of gyms. So I won Mr. Northern California in my class and became the first Chinese to win. Funnily enough, it happened to be a tie. I was already in the locker room, dressed, when it was announced.

I hurried to get my clothes back off, put on baby oil (in those days, we did not have self-tanning creams; we got tanned in the sun) on my upper body, and did a few push ups and sit ups "to pump myself up" before going onstage. I really did not have much time, which was nerve wracking, but as soon as I got onstage, I said to myself, I am going to beat this *bok guai* (white guy). That *bok guai* happened to be one of Jack LaLanne's students, but I was full of confidence and desire to prove that I was better. I knew I could do it.

And it seemed to me that at that moment the judges saw something that I had not had ten to fifteen minutes before. And that something gave me the extra point I needed to take first prize. Either it was my level of confidence and determination, or I was just better than my competitor. I do not know. The only thing that I know was that I wanted to win, and I won.

But anyway, who really was the first bodybuilder, and what is bodybuilding? Bodybuilding did not really exist prior to the late nineteenth century, when it was promoted by a man from Prussia named Eugen Sandow, who is now generally referred to as the "Father of Modern Bodybuilding." He is credited as being a pioneer of the sport because he allowed an audience to enjoy viewing his physique in "muscle display performances."

Bodybuilding is the process of maximizing muscle hypertrophy through the combination of weight training, sufficient caloric intake, and rest. Through competitive bodybuilding, bodybuilders display their physiques to a panel of judges, who assign points based on their aesthetic appearance. The muscles are revealed through a combination of fat loss, oils, and tanning which, combined with lighting, makes the definition of the muscle groups more distinct.

The roots of bodybuilding go all the way back to ancient Greece. The athletes of ancient Greece used to train in the gymnasiums; however, they did not use resistance training as a form of body modification but rather a means to improve at the sport they participated in. The most notable of such athletes was Olympic wrestling champion Milo of Croton, who would carry a calf on his back every day until it became a bull, thus demonstrating progressive resistance as a means of developing strength.

But it wasn't until the eleventh century, in India, when bodybuilding really arrived. Back then, men would lift a stone version of the dumbbell to see which man had the most stamina.

The early years of Western bodybuilding are considered to be the period between 1880 and 1930. The period from around 1940 to 1970 is often referred to as the "Golden Age" of bodybuilding because of changes in the aesthetic for more mass, as well as muscular symmetry and definition. This was due in large part to the advent of World War II, which inspired many young men to become bigger, stronger, and more aggressive in their attitudes. This was accomplished by improved training techniques, better nutrition, and more effective equipment.

If you are in good shape and work out regularly, at least three times a week, you can be prepared to enter your first contest within six months. I trained two hours, three times a week for three months to get ready for a championship. I did not have much free time. I had to run a business. But I think about six to eight months is a reasonable time frame to gain the lean mass your body needs to sustain itself as you enter the fat-burning phase of your diet, which takes place about three to four months before your contest. If you want to compete as a light-weight, for instance, you might need to be a maximum of around 160 pounds before you begin your fat-burning phase.

Personally, I never weighed more than 150 pounds, and my usual weight is 130 pounds, which is exactly the same weight I would have been when I entered a competition.

The reason why you gain weight is simple. When you go into the fat-burning phase, you will lose about one pound of muscle for every three pounds of fat. Therefore, the first thing you need to do is to decide which weight class you want to compete in and the date of the contest. Then you plan your diet.

Bodybuilding takes a lot of time in the gym and in the kitchen. Your lifestyle is built around workouts and meals ideally averaging one every three hours with at least one gram of protein for each pound of your body weight when you are trying to put on lean mass.

For example, for breakfast I would eat three egg whites (protein) and one whole egg, plus one cup of oatmeal. This was Jack LaLanne's typical breakfast as well. (Later, we learned about cholesterol and how bad it can be for your health, but in the early days I had a few raw eggs mixed with something for the flavor, plus a glass of half-and-half in the morning).

In the mid-morning, I would have fish, and at lunch, beef stew or a palm-sized fresh steak (my favorite), a sweet potato, and a bowl of vegetables. And for dinner, chicken with a lot of vegetables. (Also, do not forget that you need to drink about a half-gallon to one gallon of water daily to prevent dehydration between workouts.)

This diet is designed to put on about a pound of lean mass a week. Lots of protein, lots of carbs, and a little fat are needed to build muscles. Weight training causes micro-tears to the muscles being trained; this is generally known as micro-trauma. These micro-tears in the muscle contribute to the soreness felt after exercise, referred to as delayed onset muscle soreness. It is the repair to this micro-trauma that results in muscle growth. Normally, this soreness becomes most apparent a day or two after a workout. However, as muscles become adapted to the exercises, soreness tends to decrease.

The high levels of muscle growth and repair achieved by bodybuilders require a specialized diet. Generally speaking, bodybuilders require more calories than the average person of the same weight to support the protein and energy requirements needed for their training to increase muscle mass.

Your diet changes as you get closer to your competition day. It is a common practice for most bodybuilders to make muscle gains for most of the first three to four months, which is called the "off-season" phase. While you are adding lean mass for muscle building, you will work out with heavier weights and lower reps. And approximately three to four months from competition, you'll attempt to lose body fat by entering the fat-burning, or "cutting," phase, where you work to make your muscles more defined. By doing this, some muscle will be lost, but the aim is to keep this to a minimum. Minimizing muscle loss involves reducing calories and carb intake while increasing cardio. During this phase, you gradually work out with lighter weights and higher reps. And during your final two weeks of training before a show, you will use light weights and only "pump up" your muscles during your workouts, along with doing moderate cardio.

Almost no one talks about it, but in my workouts I began with visualization. You must know what you want and what results you are aiming for in your visualization. You should have a clear picture of how your muscles should look. You can get this picture by looking at photos of top bodybuilders in magazines.

That was one of the reasons that we hung pictures of bodybuilders at Yarik's gym — so you could see them as often as possible to create the perfect picture of your body in your mind.

In as much detail as possible, I imagined the whole process of muscle growth. I saw myself warming up, stretching, concentrating on everything that was important for working out. Then I told myself, "I am strong and ready," and I began my workout!

Following ten minutes of stretching and calisthenics, I would go to the Olympic barbell, slowly lean down, and take a shoulder-width grip, as if the barbell were an extension of my arms. Bending my knees, visualizing the whole exercise, I would squat down in front of the resistance and, with one quick snap of my arms and a thrust from my legs, in one continuous move, I would exhale, bringing the barbell to my chest. Then I stood up. After a deep inhale, briefly pausing, I would forcefully exhale and thrust the barbell to arms' length overhead, pause briefly again, and at a snail's pace I would bring it back down to the top of my chest, slowly inhaling and taking another short respite. Then I would end by lowering the barbell back to the floor, to its starting position. I could feel the pulse of blood pumping in my muscles, throughout my body. With absolutely no break, I would launch the second repetition of the movement and continue until I had completed twelve repetitions. Subsequently, after a short rest, in order to take full advantage of the cardio-respiratory and strength-building benefits, I did another two sets. I kept full mental focus on the exercise and on the muscle groups I was exercising.

Next, I had another short rest and worked on my legs and calves. Squats were the cornerstone of my barbell training. I had tried different variations of this exercise but always came back to the standard fashion. Resting a barbell across my shoulders with my feet approximately shoulder-width apart and making sure I was properly balanced, I inhaled and slowly descended to a full squat position. With no pause in the bottom position, I would then immediately return — using the strength of all of the muscles in my lower extremities — to the starting position, exhaling as I came up. Then I would perform twelve repetitions after a short rest to catch my breath, return and re-shoulder the barbell for one more set of twelve reps.

Then, lying down on a flat bench, taking a shoulder-width grip on an Olympic barbell, I began to press the weight off the support pins to arms' length above my chest. From this locked-out position, I would inhale and slowly lower the barbell to my chest and, exhaling, press it back up to its starting position, always exhaling at the time of maximum exertion. Another twelve repeats and then, after a brief break, I'd return to the bench for one more set of twelve reps. (The last two of twelve usually are the hardest ones — my muscles were tired to the point that I could barely hold the weight). I had to focus to find the strength to do the final two reps: the eleventh and the twelfth.

In physics we learn that for every action, there is a reaction. Therefore, you must gradually increase your weight, being careful not to injure yourself.

Barbell curls were also a core movement in my weight training routine to build up my biceps. To perform this movement properly, I took a comfortable shoulder-width grip on the barbell with my palms facing forward. Keeping a slight bend in my knees for stability, I then contracted my biceps and curled the barbell up to a point even with my upper pecs. Breaking off briefly in this fully-contracted position, I would steadily lower the barbell back to the starting position. After that, I would do ten minutes of posing and twenty minutes of cardio. That was my workout routine — two hours, three times a week, full-body.

My advice is that when you start to exercise, you do it mainly to keep yourself physically fit and mentally alert, to develop some degree of coordination between brain, breath and body, and to provide healthful stimulation of blood; it will be more enjoyable and less tiresome. You should develop the mental attitude of a person who does it for health benefit to avoid any issues with your well-being later on, always remembering that any form of physical training is a two-edged sword; it can cut you both ways. Remember, the human body can adapt to many things, but do not abuse it. You can go against nature for weeks, months, even years, but in the end, nature will collect its just due.

Do not fall for advertising or programs promising that you'll build a great body using muscle enhancement pills or any "magic systems" promising quick results. No pill or system is perfect, nor is any pill or system better than the person using it. It all depends on you and your willingness to succeed. This is the only key to success in building a great physique. Back then, we did not have protein powder, and steroids had not yet been invented, and yet we were able to build big muscles. Steve Reeves is proof of this.

Each week I tried to mix up my workout routine so my muscle groups stayed "surprised" and my muscles didn't get used to a fixed routine. I mixed machines with dumbbells and never did the same thing twice in a row.

A little trick I'll mention: For one week before a contest, your diet should be mostly water — one to two gallons a day. Try drinking spring water, since it has minerals your body needs. You can begin increasing water and sodium intake at the same time to deregulate the systems in the body associated with water flushing. Reducing carbohydrate consumption will deplete the muscles of glycogen (stored carbohydrates in the muscles, so to speak). When you drink this much liquid, you are flushing out your system and removing subcutaneous fluids. Then, the last two days prior to a competition, you reduce your sodium intake by half, and then eliminate it completely, because one gram of salt attracts three grams of water. Then you'll re-introduce carbohydrates into the diet to expand the muscles. This is typically known as "carb-loading." The end result is an ultra-lean body with full, hard muscles and a dry, vascular appearance. I had great results with this training regimen.

Breathing is a very valuable and often overlooked function of the human body. When you inhale, you take in oxygen, which gets transported through blood cells. When you exhale, you get rid of toxins and gases, such as carbon dioxide. Proper breathing during exercise is of utmost importance because it helps oxygenate hard-working muscles and supplies them with nutrient-rich blood.

Use proper breathing while lifting weights, and exhale when exerting the most force. To put it simply: Breathing during exertion is critically important in preventing internal injury such as hernia, blood vessel strain, and high blood pressure.

Master the art of low abdominal breathing during cardiovascular exercise. Breathe in through your nose and out through your mouth. Keep your abdomen relaxed and take deep breaths, expanding your abdomen before slowly exhaling. Continue this breathing pattern for the duration of your cardio session.

Many experts will say that to fully oxygenate the muscles and clear the body of carbon dioxide (CO_2) you should do full inhales and full exhales. You will notice a lower heart rate as you are able to get more oxygen in and, more importantly, push all the CO_2 out of your body. The CO_2 in your body will increase if your breathing patterns are short and hurried. This will increase your heart rate and lactic acid production and decrease your endurance in any cardiovascular event.

When exercising, never hold your breath, as this can put too much strain on your heart. Basically, for bodybuilding purposes your body needs increased oxygen and water to burn fat as an energy source. As you add more oxygen and water to your system, your body will be able to use the retained water for excretion, prompting almost immediate weight loss of retained water and toxins. This is not the same as sitting in a sauna and sweating, which actually dehydrates you. Adding water will rehydrate you and enable the body to burn more fat (as long as you increase your oxygen intake by doing some form of exercise). Muscle stimulation occurs in the gym, lifting weights, but muscle growth occurs afterward, during rest. Adequate rest, including sleep and recuperation between workouts, is very crucial. Without adequate rest and sleep, muscles do not have an opportunity to recover and build.

About eight hours of sleep a night is desirable for the bodybuilder to be refreshed, although this varies from person to person. Additionally, many athletes find a daytime nap further increases their body's ability to build muscle.

Another point: Posing is one of the most important elements of bodybuilding and in many cases is neglected. That is why it was in my regimen. Competitors with a well-muscled and cut body can lose to a challenger with less muscle who is nevertheless better able to show the judges what they have. From the moment you step onto the stage, you are being judged, and every muscle in your body must remain flexed. Every pose is built from the legs up. If you are doing a side chest and your legs are not flexed, your upper body will look great while your legs and calves will look flat. You will lose points.

In bodybuilding, the judges are looking for your flaws. As a bodybuilder, you are looking to hide those flaws. Posing is hard work. During a bodybuilding competition, the audience and judges are looking at you while you are standing on stage wearing nothing more than a skimpy posing suit. This is why, prior to performing on stage, I spent a lot of time in the sun to make my skin look darker, which improves muscle definition, and I used baby oil to make it shiny. While posing onstage during a bodybuilding competition, your cuts and muscularity must show up well against the very bright stage lights. You look your best if you are very dark. If your skin is not dark enough, you look washed out and flat.

While you are trying to show off your physique, your overall appearance, including grooming, is very important, too. If you are not well-groomed, it will take away from your overall look. A male bodybuilder cannot have chest hair, underarm hair, or leg hair.

Well, back then, that was my routine for getting myself ready for competition. Little did I know then that Jack LaLanne and I would live long into our nineties and become friends. I have the highest regard for him as a great person who revolutionized the health fitness industry. Also, little did I know back then that life would give me the gift of meeting another great person who would become an iconic figure throughout the world, and that I would have the honor to call him my friend.

His name was Bruce Lee.

At the beginning of WWII; please note the round pin that says "Chinese American" on the left lapel of my high school graduation suit.

A page from my war-time photo album, showing me in New Guinea.

Another page from my war-time photo album, showing Annie.

One more page from my war-time photo album.

In my Army tent in New Guinea, WWII, looking at Annie's picture.

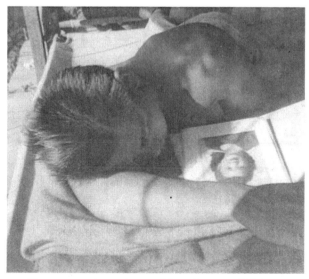

Dreaming about Annie. New Guinea, WWII.

My drawing of Annie's engagement ring with my after-war plans.

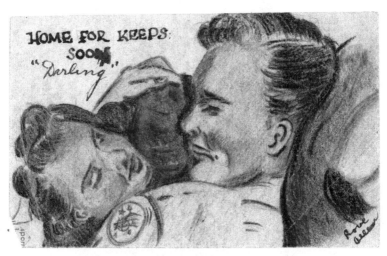

Another drawing I did of Annie and me
when we would meet after the war.

My war-time letters that were kept by Annie all these years. On the envelopes you can see my drawings with war censorship seals in the left bottom corner.

In front of a B-24 bomber at my Air Force base, WWII.

At the U.S. Air Force base in New Guinea, WWII, on the wing of a P-39 fighter plane.

In my Air Force uniform, with my mother, after I came back from the war. Oakland, California.

Newlyweds. Annie and me after our honeymoon trip to L.A.

With George Lee on my right; Bruce Lee and James Yimm Lee.
Bruce Lee Foundation photo archive

James' birthday party: I'm on the far left (in the back); James is in the middle; and Bruce is in the striped T-shirt on the far right.

Another snapshot from James's birthday party. James blows out the candles of his birthday cake after making his wish. I'm on the left, behind James, with Bruce next to him on the right.

Oakland years. I am with Linda and her son Brandon.

With Bruce in my store, Allen's Market.
Bruce Lee Foundation photo archive

The Four Musketeers. From left to right:
George, Bruce, James, and me.
On the set of *The Green Hornet* (TV series), 1966.
Bruce Lee Foundation photo archive

Clowning with Bruce.
On the set of *The Green Hornet* (TV series), 1966.
Bruce Lee Foundation photo archive

With Jack LaLanne (second from the right), his wife, and Darryl Chan (personal trainer for Bruce Lee's son, Brandon), at the San Francisco Bay Club.

All together. With Annie (she points to Brandon and Bruce's portraits) and Linda at our home in Fremont. Our dog, Sifu, is visible at bottom right.

Shannon gets a hug from her "Uncle Allen." Note the jade ring on my right hand; that's the same ring Annie gave me before I went to war.

Teaching Linda how to do the Iron Cross on gymnastic rings.

Shannon holds a scroll, while Linda stands with me at the podium during one of the Bruce Lee seminars.

Waikiki Beach in Hawaii. Annie and I renew our wedding vows.

Surrounded by family at my 90th birthday. Back row: My daughter-in-law, Stephanie Joe; son, Darrell Joe; granddaughter Denise Fong; and son-in-law Dennis Fong. Middle row: Granddaughters Emily Joe and Kristina Joe; Annette Joe Fong, my second daughter; Donna Joe Martin, my eldest daughter; Cathy L. Fong with her husband Ryan Fong, my first grandchild. Front row: Annie and I, holding hands.

Chapter 5

Friendship: "All for One, One for All"

> What is a friend? A single soul dwelling in two bodies.
>
> — Aristotle

Silver Dragon — that was our favorite restaurant to eat at. We were walking on the streets of Oakland Chinatown. The sun was playing in the windows of local shops and was blinding our eyes. We talked over the noise of passing trucks. At the same time, we were looking around, avoiding bumping into people as we practiced martial arts.

"Shin man," Bruce Lee said, laughing. He called me "Shin Man" after I kicked him in the shin. We were having fun.

That morning he had showed up at my home unannounced, in his usual surprise style. I was always happy to see him. Annie opened the door. Then he used his usual jokey greeting. He pulled his shirt up, showing off his washboard abdominal muscles, and said, "Annie, look how hard I am."

And Annie said, "Bruce, I am tired of that same joke!" She hid a smile and then gave him a hug.

When Bruce first came to Oakland, he made the decision that he would achieve a washboard stomach — which meant a stomach so lean that the well-developed muscles under the skin showed in ridges like an old-fashioned washboard used to scrub clothes. Bruce told James and me that he would have washboard abs in six weeks. He used to lift his shirt whenever he saw us during those six weeks, showing his progress. And he did it. That was how focused and determined Bruce was, and yet he was so much fun to be around.

Oh, he had millions of jokes, every time a new one. Bruce was the funniest guy I knew. And he was about to become one of the most famous individuals of the last decades of the 20th century, creating a pop-culture of martial arts throughout the world.

The most famous individuals always have an inner circle of friends and trusted advisers who are willing to provide counsel, share opinions, and support them in accomplishing goals. Bruce liked to clown around a lot but he was a man who picked his friends carefully, surrounding himself with only the most sincere people.

Now, after all those years, I have met many good people who became great friends, but I will always remember James, George, and Bruce. Bruce's inner circle of friends — we were the Four Musketeers; that was what people called us.

It all began with my long time friend, James Yimm Lee. Now, let me tell you a little bit about him. During high school, just like I did, he practiced weight training, bodybuilding, hand balancing, and acrobatics. But as I mentioned before, James was always one step ahead of me. We shared the same interests, passions, and hobbies, but he was always the first. I would start something without any knowledge of him doing it, only to realize later on that he had already done it. We got so used to it that I stopped being surprised when he and I bumped into each other when we least expected it.

James was a very popular guy. In elementary school, students voted him class president. He was a few years older than I was, and I looked up to him. His family had a shrimp business in Oakland Chinatown, which also served as a gambling joint in the back room. Visiting him, I ran into Tong men, gang members; they were always playing Chinese lottery tickets. As I became older I found out the Tong were gung fu men as well. That was how I learned what gung fu is. Later on, it would become James' and my life-long passion.

James and I both liked weight training. In 1938, James was already on the Oakland YMCA weightlifting team and won the Northern California Championship in the light weight division.

Although James had an avid talent for drawing and art just as I did, he became a welder and got a job at the Pearl Harbor shipyards in Hawaii. It was there, when James started studying Judo at the Okazaki Gym and competing in a few amateur boxing matches, the attack on Pearl Harbor happened and World War II began.

After surviving the bombing of Pearl Harbor, James returned to Oakland and continued welding until he entered the Army. When James was stationed in the Philippines, he got infected with malaria. But his condition became so serious that James was shipped to the death ward. There, he continued to fight the disease. James was a fighter in the deepest sense of that word. The illness caused him to lose almost forty percent of his body weight, resulting in a disability which he never tried to exploit or use as an excuse. In April 1946, he was discharged and came back home. Determined to regain his strength, James began weight training.

He exercised every day; gradually he regained his strength and started martial arts training at Sil Lum Gung Fu in San Francisco. I started my training as well, but in Oakland. In four years, James became known for his iron hand training, performing public demonstrations of breaking ten bricks with his bare hands. No one ever knew that he was a disabled war veteran. James had developed an incredibly powerful punch. Yet his hands were not calloused; they were soft and smooth. James used to make his own oils so his hands would look like a gentleman's hands.

Between 1957 and 1958, he authored, published, and distributed by mail order through his own company, Oriental Book Sales, a book series called *Modern Kung-Fu Karate: Iron, Poison Hand Training*. James was very serious about what he was doing, but he still liked to joke and have a good time. With his personality of a street fighter and philosopher, he always reminded me of Bruce.

James was already an established and respected instructor of gung fu and iron hand training in Oakland, California, when he met Bruce. His older brother, Bob, and his friend, George Lee, were watching a dancing competition at the Chinese Association of Dancers in San Francisco where Bruce Lee was performing Hong Kong style Cha Cha dancing. During intermission, he showed his martial arts skills.

"There is something that you have to see," Bob and George both told James when they came to visit him at home next day. The two of them were fired up about their dancing instructor and his fighting style.

"We never saw anything like that before," they said, trying to convince him. He was convinced. James was intrigued with Bruce. (Bob and George had also told Bruce about James's unique martial arts skills, so Bruce was as intrigued with James as James was with him). James asked me to "check out this cat" since it happened that I was going on a family trip and would stay a few days in Seattle to attend the World's Fair in the summer of 1962.

Nearly 10 million people came to the fair. The U.S. government, for its part, was exceedingly interested in demonstrating the nation's scientific prowess to the world and therefore committed over nine million dollars to the fair, chiefly to build the NASA-themed

United States Science Exhibit. A number of foreign governments provided the international flavor crucial to a World's Fair, and eventually thirty-five states signed on as exhibitors.

President John F. Kennedy officially opened the Fair on April 21, 1962. He spoke by telephone from Palm Beach, Florida, where he was spending his Easter holidays. "I am honored to open the Seattle World's fair today," he said. "What we show is achieved with great effort in the fields of science, technology, and industry. These accomplishments are a bridge which carries us confidently towards the twenty-first century. Many nations have sent exhibits and will send their people. We welcome them."

This exemplifies the spirit of peace and cooperation with which we approached the decades ahead — again in John F. Kennedy's words: "May we open not only a great World's fair; may we also open an era of peace and understanding among all mankind. Let the fair begin!"

After that speech, I told myself I had to see it. So, I closed my store and took Annie and the kids to Seattle.

The extravagant opening ceremony began with 538 clanging bells, 2000 balloons, and ten Air Force F-102 fighters swooping overhead. It was simply breathtaking. For the next six months, visitors would be entertained not just by the many exhibits, but also by an array of musicians, orchestras, dance troupes, art collections, singers, comedians, and other various shows traveling through the fair during its run.

Vice-President Lyndon Johnson, Walt Disney, and Prince Phillip of Great Britain visited the exposition as guests; adding to the star-studded atmosphere was the presence of the King of Rock and Roll, Elvis Presley, who arrived to shoot a film at the same time in Seattle. It was a magical place, filled with multi-colored lights, wonderful sights, and exciting rides. The Space Needle, the Monorail, the Science Center, and the Amusement Park were thrilling! Delicious food, fun times, and fond memories.

It happened that the Hotel Monticello, where I stayed in Seattle, was only half a block away from a restaurant where Bruce worked and lived. If that had not been the case, I would probably not have met Bruce; my schedule was too busy. That day, I came in late at night and had to leave early in the morning for Canada. I had practically no time. So I am pretty sure it was luck that brought Bruce and me together that night.

The name of that restaurant was Ruby Chow; the owner was Bruce Lee's family friend. It was a nice, well-established business, known for the people who worked there and lived nearby; they were Chinese movie and opera actors who had recently immigrated to America.

When I came inside. I noticed not many people were in the restaurant, and I wondered why. I looked at my watch — quarter to eleven, almost closing time. It was my second try to meet Bruce that day; I had come earlier that day but had missed him. It was his day off. I was advised to come back at night, close to eleven. I hoped that he would be there this time.

Then I saw a beautiful Chinese lady with a very elaborate Asian hairstyle and wearing an elegant oriental dress standing by the front desk.

"Hi," she said in English with a pleasant voice and a smile. It was Ruby Chow.

"Hi," I said politely, smiling back. I introduced myself. "I am here to see Bruce Lee." I waited for a second and added, "My friend from San Francisco said that he is a good martial artist."

"He is out for the evening but expected to be back soon," Ruby Chow said. She was looking for something on her desk. "In ten, fifteen minutes," she continued, writing my name down.

Well, it seemed to me that I might not be able meet him after all. But I said, "If it is only fifteen minutes, I will wait here."

"Do you care for a drink while waiting?" Ruby asked me, the good host that she was.

"Scotch, please," I said as I sat down in a chair facing an entrance door. In fifteen minutes, Ruby brought me another. "She was reading my mind," I thought. Time passed by. I was getting lonely in that empty room. More than half an hour had passed, and I was ready to leave.

But then from seemingly nowhere appeared a well-groomed young man in an iron-pressed gray flannel suit. His shoes looked like he had polished them just behind the entrance door.

It must be Bruce, was what I thought. I had never seen a man like that before. All this time I had been looking at the main entrance door, but he had used a side door; otherwise I would've spotted him right away.

He looked more like a model than a gung fu man. A handsome Asian man with an attractive face, his wide eyebrows slightly raised, defining deep, dark eyes that were glowing with some unexplainable mystery. His narrow lips seemed to be a bit feminine but his chiseled nose and chin gave him that classic Greek warrior look. He looked full of youth.

"Probably he's coming from a date," I thought when he was approaching me.

"Allen Joe?" he said.

"Bruce Lee?" I said almost at the same time.

At first Bruce was a little cautious; he had thought that Allen Joe was a Caucasian and could not understand why I wanted to see him, but as soon as he saw me and I mentioned Bob and James Lee's names, Bruce loosened up. (Years later, he said he'd thought I had come to challenge him to fight).

We continued our conversation in English; then we realized that we both spoke Cantonese, the same dialect. He was surprised. Bruce asked me to join him for a late-night hamburger and root beer. (The strongest memory for me about that night — how very friendly he was). I said that I was staying not far from there in a hotel with my family, and it was midnight; I would need to check if they were alright and let them know where I was. I invited him to meet Annie and our two daughters (we did not have our son yet).

Bruce asked to be excused. He ran upstairs to his room to change his suit. And then in two minutes he was back downstairs in a gray sweatsuit, holding notebooks in his hands. We went outside, heading toward my hotel. I had forgotten whether I had paid for my drinks or not, and that still bothers me now!

I spoke to my family; everything was okay. So Bruce and I went out for our late-night burger. The weather was nice — a warm, summer night with a clear sky, which was kind of unusual for Seattle. I was relaxed; after all, it was my vacation. When we were passing Ruby Chow's, Bruce stopped in the middle of the green grass lawn in front of the restaurant.

"Show me some gung fu," Bruce said.

"What?" I asked him.

"Show me what you've learned!"

I slowly flexed my muscles and demonstrated some of the sam seeng kune (three-line fist).

"Pretty good," said Bruce with a puzzled look on his face. "Now, throw a straight punch at me," he said, looking in my eyes.

"Okay," I said and I punched him with my right arm.

Bruce blocked and grabbed my punching hand, and in the same continuous move pulled me forward. He pulled me so hard that I lost my balance and would have fallen if he had not caught me. I was shocked by how inhumanly fast he was. Bruce was in full control, dragging me all over the place. He jerked my shoulder so hard that my socket is still sore today. But let me say this: It was the beginning of a great friendship!

At the restaurant, Bruce showed me some of his gung fu notes and drawings. He was writing a book on gung fu already. I was impressed. Bruce wanted to talk more, but I had to leave. We had agreed to meet the next morning in front of Ruby Chow's restaurant.

This time, Bruce was waiting for me. I ran across the street, and Bruce quickly walked to me and shook my hand.

"You have time?" He wanted to invite me for breakfast and then to be his guest on *You Ask for It*, a TV show that he had to appear on in the afternoon. Of course I wanted to go with him but I had promised my family to take them to Canada that day; we said goodbye, shook hands again, and I rushed back to the hotel.

When I returned to the Bay Area, the first thing I did was call James so that I could tell him that Bruce was for real.

And who was Bruce Lee? He was a young college student at the time. James was twenty years older than Bruce. Bruce Lee was born on November 27, 1940, at the Jackson Street Hospital in San Francisco's Chinatown when his parents were on a tour with an opera company in the United States. My mother was a big fan of his father, who by profession was a comedian in the Chinese opera and an actor in Cantonese films. She knew almost everything about him, and when Bruce was visiting me at my home, my mom would often stop by to talk with Bruce about opera. Anyway, it was fortuitous for Bruce's future that he was born in America so that he could return to claim his birthright of American citizenship eighteen years later.

When he was three months old, Bruce's family had returned to Hong Kong, where they lived through Japanese occupation until the British returned to power at the end of the war in 1945.

"China claims that 35 million Chinese were killed or wounded during the Japanese occupation from 1931 to 1945. An estimated 2.7 million Chinese were killed in a Japanese 'pacification' program that targeted 'all males between the ages of fifteen and sixty who were suspected to be enemies' along with other 'enemies pretending to be local people'. Out of the thousands of Chinese prisoners captured during the war, only fifty-six were found alive in 1946."[4] It was pure horror for the Chinese to live under the Japanese occupation at that time. You could be killed for no reason, or even just for fun. I never talked to Bruce about it but could only imagine what he and his family went through.

At the age of thirteen, Bruce was introduced to Master Yip Man, a teacher of the Wing Chun style of gung fu. For five years he studied diligently and became very proficient. It did not take long for Bruce to learn that the real value of martial arts training is that the skills of physical combat instill confidence to the point that one does not feel the constant need to defend one's honor through fighting. And it was probably then that the first philosophical seeds sprouted within him.

Bruce was also a terrific dancer, and in 1958 he won the Hong Kong Cha Cha Championship. That is why it was no surprise that his part-time job was as a dancing instructor when he decided to move to America. He was well-known by the Chinese Dancing Association throughout the country and was invited to numerous events.

In addition to his studies, gung fu, and dancing, Bruce had another side interest during his school years. He was a child actor who had appeared in twenty films. Bruce loved acting. And he was always looking for something new, so his family decided that it was time for him to return to the land of his birth and find his future there.

In April of 1959, with one hundred dollars in his pocket, Bruce boarded a steamship from Hong Kong on a journey to San Francisco. His passage was in the lower decks of the ship, but it didn't take long for Bruce to be invited up to the first class accommodations to teach the passengers the Cha Cha. Landing in San Francisco, Bruce was armed with the knowledge that his

---

[4] "Japanese Occupation of China Before World War II," *Jeffrey Hays*, accessed July 04, 2015. http://factsanddetails.com/asian/ca67/sub426/item2537.html.

dancing abilities might provide him a living, so that was why his first job in America was as a dance instructor.

Bruce did not stay long in San Francisco. He traveled to Seattle where a family friend, Ruby Chow, had a restaurant and had promised Bruce a job and living quarters above the restaurant. By now Bruce had left his acting and dancing passions behind and was intent on furthering his education. He enrolled at Edison Technical School where he fulfilled the requirements for the equivalent of a high school graduation before enrolling at the University of Washington.

There, he majored in philosophy. His passion for gung fu inspired a desire to develop the philosophical underpinnings of the arts.

In the three years that Bruce studied at the university, he supported himself by teaching gung fu, having by this time given up working in the restaurant. He and a few of his new friends would meet in parking lots, garages, or any open space, and play around with gung fu techniques. At that time gung fu was an unknown practice, as was karate. Naturally, Bruce's small group of friends was intrigued by this new art called gung fu.

They were the ones who encouraged him to open a school of gung fu. So Bruce rented a small basement room in Seattle's Chinatown and called his school the Jun Fan Gung Fu Institute. It was during those years a life-long relationship formed between James and Bruce when James started training directly under him. James was open-minded and decided to learn what this talented young practitioner had to offer. He contacted Bruce and they began visiting each other.

In those days Bruce's school was known as Jun Fan Gung Fu; later, he renamed it Jeet Kune Do. Bruce and James would take turns going back and forth between Seattle and Oakland for their gung fu training.

In 1963, having established a dedicated group of students and having given numerous demonstrations at the university,

Bruce thought he might attract more students by opening a larger school. So he did.

One of his students was a gorgeous freshman at the University of Washington, Linda Emery. Linda knew who Bruce was from his guest lectures in Chinese philosophy at Garfield High School, and in the summer after graduating, at the urging of her Chinese girlfriend, Linda started taking gung fu lessons. It wasn't long before the instructor became more interesting than the lessons. That too was a beginning of a beautiful relationship.

Bruce and Linda got married, and on their wedding day, they flew from Seattle and moved to Oakland. By this time, Bruce had decided to make a career out of teaching gung fu. His plan involved opening a number of schools around the country and training assistant instructors to teach in his absence.

James picked Bruce and Linda up at the airport, and they moved into his home. There, in Oakland, Bruce opened his second school with James.

The couple stayed with James and helped him with his children after James' wife, Katherine, died of breast cancer during that same year. They lived at the Oakland residence for the next two years.

James' house was built on a hill. On the ground level was the large garage, which was James' training room. The second level had three bedrooms, one of which was occupied by Bruce and Linda. James still worked as a welder at Westinghouse, while Linda kept the house. Bruce's job was to operate the gung fu school and to develop new combat techniques. Thus was the beginning of the Oakland "fighting school."

It was during this time that Bruce had that infamous fight with Wong Jack Man in Oakland.

Bruce and James had the martial arts school in Oakland (with no name to advertise its purpose). The traditional gung fu instructors in the Bay area took offense that Bruce was teaching non-Chinese students and sent an ultimatum with Wong Jack

Man and his entourage, telling him to cease at once. Wong Jack Man told Bruce Lee that if he didn't stop teaching non-Chinese students, he would come back and make him stop. To Wong's surprise Bruce immediately accepted the challenge and said, "Why wait? Let's fight now."

James slipped to the entrance door and locked it, so no one from Wong's group could leave. James was not surprised by that visit; we all knew it was bound to happen. And a very pregnant Linda was there also.

According to James, the fight lasted three minutes. Bruce got tired of chasing Wong Jack Man from one room to another, and at the end Bruce pinned him down to the floor and asked him to give up.

The traditional Kung Fu people in the area then left him alone. That evening, I was about to close my business when I got a phone call.

"It's all over; he won!" James said. I was relieved because we'd known that the fight was inevitable. The next day the Chinese newspapers were saying that it was a draw, but we did not pay too much attention to it.

Bruce was upset with himself after the fight. He realized that by using his traditional gung fu it had taken him longer than he intended to defeat Wong. At that point, he had decided to get out of his "classical mess" and reevaluate his approach. This was the beginning of what we now know as his personal evolution. Bruce Lee had developed his own version of martial arts, popularly known to the world as Jeet Kune Do, or JKD.

Almost every evening, when James got home around seven from work, Bruce would be waiting for him to practice some new technique that he had developed during the day. Linda cooked for them while Bruce and James went downstairs to the garage and spent hours developing JKD. And then they ate. I remember Linda asked me to show her how to cook Chinese food, since I was the one who helped with cooking at my house and hosted all banquets for my friends. She was eager to learn Chinese cuisine just to make Bruce happy! Linda was simply spoiling him. I think he owes her at least half of his success.

James regularly stopped by at my butcher shop to buy his groceries and have what I called his "coffee royal" — coffee with whiskey, which I kept for him in a back room at my shop. I used that room as a gym. By that time, I had expanded my business, buying the grocery store next door to my existing shop. I removed the wall that divided the two stores and blocked the entrance door, making one big room. At this point, I sold pretty much everything except hard liquors.

In the back of my store, I had two small storage rooms where I kept some inventories packed in boxes and stocked along the walls. In the middle of the first room was a reclining bench with a big safe, dumbbells (thirty and fifty pounds), and barbells (with fifteen, thirty, and fifty pound weights) on the cement floor. All of those weights were enough for me to keep myself in shape.

Through that room you could walk to a smaller one, and that was where James showed me any new moves that Bruce had just developed. At the beginning, Bruce would come to cash his checks at my store (he had just moved from Seattle and had not opened a bank account yet). He also stopped by at "my gym" anytime he wanted me to show him how to do a certain exercise to build some muscles. Then we'd talk while Bruce would enjoy an ice cold root beer. Unfortunately, at my shop I did not have his favorite brand, *A&W* — it was not as popular those days as *Hires*, but Bruce was okay with that.

After work, whenever I had time, I visited James' garage. To get inside of his garage to start your training class, you had to literally get on your hands and knees and crawl under the door to get in. The garage door was three-quarters of the way down. For students, it was the rule — not to come to the front door, but to go directly to the garage. Students came from as far as seventy miles away.

In addition to his expert gung-fu skills, James Yimm Lee was also an accomplished weightlifter and helped to get Bruce started in a weight-training program. They asked me to help in sculpting his physique, since bodybuilding was my area of expertise. Bruce always joked with me, calling me "my body."

I gave him his first set of weights (it was my way of saying thank you for teaching me his fighting style) and helped to develop a three-day-per-week bodybuilding program that fit Bruce's strengthening and bodybuilding needs. I introduced him to basic weight training techniques. The routine consisted of squats, pullovers, and curls for about three sets each — old school techniques that combined full-body workouts with half weightlifting and half bodybuilding elements. Nothing really spectacular, but we were just getting him started, and the workouts fit in perfectly with his own philosophy of getting the maximum results out of the minimum effort. In his weight training, as in his martial arts, Bruce chose what worked for him, tailoring his workouts specifically for himself. In his usual style, he observed me during my workouts, making notes and sketches.

Bruce's every-other-day workout schedule allowed for the often neglected aspect of muscle recovery to take place. I coordinated his bodybuilding workouts to ensure that they fell on days when he wasn't engaged in either endurance-enhancing or overly strenuous martial arts training. The program worked like magic, increasing his bodyweight from an initial 130 pounds to, at one point, topping out at just over 155 pounds.

He looked like a real bodybuilder.

Bruce wanted his weight training to complement what he did in martial arts. That was his main aim. A lot of what Bruce was doing was about being able to maintain arm positions that nobody could violate in a fight. For example, most people who are into bodybuilding are interested in simply building up their muscles to a bigger size, particularly the major muscle groups, and not much attention is paid to building strength in the connective tissues, like ligaments and tendons.

Well, Bruce's approach was *Let's build up the connectors, and we won't worry so much about the size of the muscle.* Again, Bruce was about function. He was able to develop incredible chest musculature. His upper pecs were impressive, bunching and splitting into thousands of fibrous bands, and his biceps had developed an incredible pulling power, which he used to such good effect in all of his sparring sessions. Focusing his training for function made him look his best. James and I were happy for him.

James had a close relationship with a number of noted martial artists: Jujitsu master Wally Jay; Shaolin Kenpo instructor Ralph Castro; and American Kenpo founder Ed Parker. He introduced Bruce to these individuals, and it was through Ed Parker that Bruce got noticed by Hollywood and eventually received a screen test, which got him the role of Kato in *The Green Hornet* television series.

James had also designed and constructed many unique training devices that he and Bruce used in their workouts. But for more difficult pieces, they asked for George Lee's help. George had worked with planes and drills, creating metal works and pieces for use with machinery.

The first time I met George was in one of El Cerrito's gyms, though I have forgotten the name of the particular gym. Back then, I liked to check out different gyms so I could borrow the best ideas for the small gym I had built at my home in Berkeley by converting a garage and outdoor room. I had a dream to have a place that was both a martial arts studio and gym. And I had opened that kind of gym, but I guess I was ahead of my time.

Anyway, in the El Cerrito gym, I spotted the only Chinese guy who was doing chin-ups. It was George. I went to him and introduced myself. We talked and to my surprise we had mutual friends — James and his older brother Bob. We laughed. I invited him to check out my "small gym." That was the beginning of another great friendship.

George was born in Monterey, California, in 1917. As I recall, when he was seven, his father sent him off to China to attend military school. It was at this school that George had his first encounter with martial arts, but it was short-lived. With the onset of war and the Japanese invasion, George returned home to California and attended Berkeley High School, becoming a machinist's apprentice.

George had met Bruce in the early 1960s in the Bay Area. He and James' older brother were taking dancing classes from a young, dynamic man teaching Hong Kong Cha Cha. That man was Bruce Lee. George would still occasionally take classes from James and Bruce. One day George noticed that Bruce kept all his loose change in an old shoebox. As a gift, George decided to fashion him some metal boxes in which Bruce could keep his change as well as files and other materials. Bruce was amazed by George's metal-working talent. He asked if George could fashion some training equipment and, from there, a creative partnership began.

Bruce sketched things for George to make; the completed product often took a bit of trial and error to get it just right. The first thing George made for Bruce was a pair of his famous nunchucks. Bruce sketched them on a napkin, and George went to work.

The creation of nunchucks is a great example of how the two worked together to perfect their products. Bruce tried out the first set of nunchucks George made and found they were too long, so George shortened them from fourteen inches to twelve inches. Also, the nunchucks were a bit awkward because they were not tapered but straight wooden cylinders. George tapered them, and then for grip and flair, three rings were etched around the base of each bar – a design which has been copied over and over and is standard to this day. George also strengthened the chain from its original brass to stainless steel and made some modifications to the pin which attached the chain to the wooden dowel.

That was how it worked – Bruce would sketch, George would forge, and the two would refine the design together. Every time I visited George at his home he would show me something new that they had worked on. In those days I met him often, since his youngest son had started dating my oldest daughter.

As I remember, he made approximately fourteen pieces of equipment for Bruce. However, George fashioned many things other than training equipment, such as desk nameplates, a brass bowl, pins, and calling cards. But the creation that he and Bruce especially cherished was the small tombstone symbolizing the death of the "classical" martial artist.

As Bruce progressed in his strength and training, the equipment also progressed. Modifications within something new were always taking place. All four of us had artistic skills; we designed, sketched, and built things with our hands. But George was different; he had craftsmanship skills.

All of us had so much in common — the same interests, same hobbies. After awhile we could understand each other without even saying a single word — we just enjoyed being together.

George always said that Bruce helped him to change his attitude. He had previously suffered from having a short fuse. Bruce taught him to walk away, to avoid a confrontation. George would ask, "But what if someone spits in my face?"

And Bruce would calmly say, "Just wipe it off and walk away." James and I laughed.

But I think what George learned from Bruce helped him to become inwardly stronger. We all admired Bruce for his wisdom.

After Bruce moved to Los Angeles, James, George, and I visited him there. Bruce would teach us new moves that he had developed. I never dreamed that martial arts could be so effective in the way Bruce taught it.

That was the thing about him. Bruce was one in a million. He was always doing something. But there was never a dull moment with him.

I remember that during one visit in L.A. Bruce talked me into changing my hairstyle. I had long, thick hair that fell down my neck, and he was trying to convince me to cut it really short to look like him. Bruce told me, "I will treat you to a haircut."

"I don't know," I replied, looking into a mirror at my long hair and knowing that my wife would not like the idea.

Bruce was insistent. He went on, "My hairstylist cuts the hair of Hollywood celebrities."

That fact was very tempting — to look like a celebrity...

"Okay," I said, and looked in the mirror for the last at my long hair.

Long story short, when I came home, the first thing that my daughter Donna told me was, "Daddy, what have you done to your hair?" My wife gazed at me and burst out laughing. She just could not help herself: I looked way too extravagant, with my ears embarrassingly exposed.

Bruce and I had fun every time. We used to eat out together, always Chinese food. Bruce's favorite meal was oyster sauce beef with rice and vegetables on the side and, of course, root beer. Bruce would flip a coin for who would pay at the end of the meal. Maybe I wouldn't have had to pay so often if it weren't for Bruce's sleight-of-hand tricks!

James helped Bruce Lee publish his first book, *Chinese Gung-Fu: The Philosophical Art of Self-Defense*. And after Bruce moved to Los Angeles in 1966, James continued to teach in his garage. The chief reason that Bruce turned his attention to acting was that he had lost interest in spreading his way of martial arts in a wide-scale manner. He had begun to see that if his schools became more numerous, he would lose control of the quality of the teaching. Bruce loved his students. They were like members of his family. His love for martial arts was not something that he wanted to turn into a business.

In 1966, production started on *The Green Hornet*. The filming lasted for six months, which was for one season, and that was the end of it. When they first started filming, the cameras were not able to record the fight scenes clearly because of Bruce's speed. They asked him to slow down to capture the action. Bruce's gung fu moves thrilled audiences, and the series became a sought-after collector item in later years.

No matter how busy Bruce was, he had always found time to call or visit us when he was in the Bay Area. Bruce would stop at my house for dinner, and we would eat and talk, and on occasion he would dance the Cha Cha for us. My children loved when he danced. I remember when my oldest daughter, Donna, told me about the very first time she and her sister, Annette, saw Bruce in Seattle, when she was a little girl; they were standing quietly behind the corner of the Monticello Hotel and wondering, "Who is that handsome-looking man our daddy is talking to?" I think back then both of them were secretly in love with Bruce.

My children, Donna, Annette, and Darrell — they were everything to me. They were the reason I asked my wife not to take a job and to stay home with our kids, instead, so they would be well brought-up children; I wanted to make sure that they had good grades at school. As incentives, my wife and I would take them to nice restaurants every time we went out together. Bruce knew about this, and during one of his Christmas visits he promised my oldest daughter, Donna, that he would take her to a restaurant when she turned twenty-one. Donna could not wait for her twenty-first birthday. My wife and I still smile when we recall Bruce's kind offer.

Well, nothing had changed since he left Oakland — except for his new fans, who would crowd the block that I lived on. It was the same Bruce, though; fame did not change his personality. We were still good friends.

To me, friendship is one of the most important things in my life. Real friends love you no matter what. My friends are a family. A true friend is an extension of you — of your soul. Friends teach each other. They are compassionate, patient, and forgiving with each other; friends provide wisdom and are ready to sacrifice for each other. In our loyalty to each other, we built honor and respect. For George, James, Bruce, and me loyalty was not just a lot of words — it was a way of life.

Famous individuals always have a trusted circle of friends — and if they are lucky, they have a partner who supports them. For Bruce Lee, that partner was Linda. I remember the first time I saw her, which was in my store. The door opened and there stood a tall, slim girl with big, beautiful, blue eyes hesitantly looking at me.

"May I help you?" I asked.

"Hi, I'm Linda, Bruce's wife," she said quietly as she came toward me. I don't remember what I said after that or what she said to me. What I am still able to bring to mind is how quiet and shy Linda was. She was only nineteen.

After that first meeting, Linda would often come to my store to buy groceries and cash Bruce's checks. Today, I regret that I did not save any of those checks — now they could be an interesting addition to Bruce's museum exposition. These were ten-and twenty-dollar checks that he got for giving dancing lessons.

My store was a meeting place for all of us. Annie had just given a birth to our son, and we were in the process of moving from our two-bedroom house in Berkeley to a new place I'd bought in Fremont. We needed more room and space for our growing family.

When we started having children, Annie left her secretarial position in our local school district and became a full-time mom. So Annie stayed home and took care of the children while I ran my business and spent my free time to be with them as much as I could — that was a promise I had made to myself when I was ten years old, after my father left. I told myself that when I had children I would be always there for them so they would not experience what I had gone through as a child.

In my store, I learned all the news about what was going on in my friends' lives. They stopped by to visit me, spend time together, and buy food. A year after the birth of Annie's and my son, Linda and Bruce had their first son, Brandon. He was born in the same hospital where my three children — Donna, Annette, and Darrell — had been born. After that, I saw Linda much more often, since she came in on a regular basis to buy baby formula for Brandon at my store. It was not an easy time for her — she was taking care of her baby and helping James with his children because James' wife had just passed away. But I was amazed at Linda's transformation from a shy girl to a strong woman. When James lost his wife soon after they'd bought their new home, Bruce and Linda had moved there to take care of him and his children. It was hard for James. We were all there for our friend.

Time went so fast. Soon Linda and Bruce moved to L.A. and gave birth to their second child, a girl named Shannon. All of us went to L.A. to see her. I never saw Bruce look so good and so happy. He met us with his shirt off, holding his baby girl in his arms. Now Shannon is a mother herself, but for me Shannon will always be Bruce's little girl.

We were all happy for Bruce and Linda. From L.A. they went to Hong Kong so that Bruce could achieve the dream of his life — to make movies. After Bruce completed his contract with Golden Harvest, a production company in Hong Kong, and then became a bankable commodity, he was able to have more input into the quality of his films.

For his third film, Bruce was not only a star actor but was able to direct and produce, as well. Once again, the film broke records. Now Hollywood was listening. Warner Bros. asked him to start filming *Enter the Dragon*. It was the first ever Hong Kong-American co-production, and it was a turning point in Hong

Kong's film industry. It represented Bruce's victory in Hollywood after, only few years before, they had refused to offer him the role of the wise man in a television series set in the Old West, featuring an Eastern monk who roamed the countryside solving problems. Instead, the role had gone to David Carradine, despite the fact that the show had been Bruce's idea. The series was *Kung Fu*. But the studio claimed that a Chinese man was not a profitable star at that time.

Hugely disappointed, Bruce sought other ways to break down studio doors. He finally succeeded, and history was made: Bruce was the first Asian actor playing a star role in Hollywood. That was only the beginning. Back then, I did not know that Bruce would become a global icon influencing the minds of millions, becoming that invisible bridge connecting West and East. Or that his influence would be found in movies, art, music, fashion — in practically everything and everywhere. The only thing I wonder is how one man could accomplish that much. What was his secret?

Of course, all of that was later. But the same year, in 1972, James published his book, *Wing Chun Kung Fu*, with Bruce as the book's technical editor. James was getting ready to visit Bruce in Hong Kong but then died suddenly and unexpectedly. We all knew that he had lung cancer, and because of that he'd had to spend few days in the hospital, but doctors had said that he was feeling better and had discharged him.

Right before that, I had met him in a restaurant, and he was ordering lobsters, making jokes, just like his regular self. Then I got a note from him in the mail saying, "Dear Tiger —" that was what he called me "— I feel better and I am going back to weight training. This week, I am getting back in shape to teach JKD again. See you soon! Jimmy."

He often sent me those kind of notes. Nothing seemed out of the ordinary to me. But that turned to be the last note that I received from him. James died in the bathtub while taking shower at his home. He was fifty-two.

Later on, Linda told me that Bruce had cried when he learned that James had died, and that this was the only time she'd seen him cry. James and Bruce had been so close.

It was not easy for George and me, either. We did not want to accept that James was no longer with us. That same year, I sold my business; everything in that store reminded me of James.

I got a new job at a supermarket and was trying to get used to losing James. Then one day I got a phone call from Annie.

"Bruce died," she said, as if it were a question, not a statement.

I felt as if the ground had moved from under my feet. I was in shock. We had just spoken with him on the telephone not long ago.

Bruce was only thirty-two when he died. The world lost a brilliant star and an evolved, beautiful human being that day. His spirit remains an inspiration to untold numbers of people around the world.

Bruce had died just seven months after James. Everything felt like a slow-motion movie to me. I called George and Linda, wired money to buy flowers for Bruce's funeral in Hong Kong. I could barely comprehend what I was doing.

When you unexpectedly lose someone close to you, it feels as if you've lost a part of yourself. You used to talk, do certain things together — you had a routine that you depended on and yet at the same time didn't think too much about until that someone leaves you. You are not yourself without that person. That's how I felt after I lost two best friends, James and Bruce. I felt a kind of vacuum, an empty space that I could never fill again. But Linda — Bruce's wife — helped me feel whole again.

That's how our friendship really began. As time passed, we became like one family. I made sure that no one would harm Linda and Bruce's little girl, Shannon. And they started calling me Uncle Allen. They knew that someone was always there to help.

Time healed the pain of loss, and at that juncture in our life we had decided that something had to be done to protect what Bruce had started when he was alive. That was what brought to life the idea of Bruce Lee's Foundation. To us, it was a significant way to make an everlasting impact for generations to come.

The years rolled by. George reached his ninety-fifth birthday. The last week of his life, I talked to him over the phone every day.

I am not a religious man but every morning when I wake up I say a prayer for all of them, my friends. Then I say thank you to "The Man Upstairs," make a cup of strong coffee, then exercise, and it is like a tradition to me now — when I exercise the last two of twelve reps (the most difficult reps because muscles are already tired) I find the strength and do them: the eleventh for "The Man Upstairs" and the twelfth for my friend Bruce Lee. After that I make breakfast, and wake up the love of my life, Annie, so we can eat together. Then Annie turns on her two tablets and iPad that we use to check emails and go onto Facebook — to be connected with our children, and to the world.

As a founding member and part of the board of directors of Bruce Lee's Foundation, I still often travel to seminars, meet young people, and help them discover potential within themselves to reach their goals. I am what survives of me. I want to leave behind not what is going to be engraved on my tombstone but what is going to be woven into the lives of others. I cannot leave a better legacy to the world than my family, my beliefs, and my practices. Every day is important to me. I feel that I must finish what George, James, and Bruce began back then. We wanted to create a world that is a better place for you.

That is our legacy for you!

Epilogue

The Torch

Now that I have begun living life in my nineties, whenever I start meeting interesting and motivated people like you, it inspires me to continue to make a difference in this life — to live a fulfilling life and be happy.

I survived war, dengue fever, and cancer. And looking back I was searching for an answer — what helped me to overcome all that? And the answer is friendship and love. I was not alone. I was surrounded by friends and good people. I had survived because of love. The love of my wife, Annie. Her love and her jade ring that she gave to me, which, like a guardian angel, shielded me in the war. With her letters, she had supported me in the most critical moments of my life. I knew that I was loved. I had to come back home because my Annie was waiting for me.

I always believed in miracles, and miracles happened. I am the living testament of it. What chance did I have to find that jade ring in the jungle — probably not more than meeting Bruce in that Seattle restaurant, right? But it happened, both things did. And then what chance did Bruce have to change the lives of millions and become known throughout the world? But it happened.

The greatest values to me are my family and friends. Through all these years, it has been my biggest privilege to be a friend of Bruce Lee and be to called Uncle Allen by his wife Linda and their daughter Shannon. I would not exchange that love for anything in the world. I will remain their uncle for as long as I live.

My advice to you is this: Believe in yourself and exercise every day. I am ninety-two years old and I have never stopped exercising. It keeps my body, mind, and spirit strong.

It is my pleasure to share this story with you. I hope this story and this book will inspire you to live a life that will make you proud of yourself. I want you to be the next person who picks up our torch, the one whose story will inspire millions. I hope to meet you and shake your hand.

I am not saying goodbye. I am saying, "Until we meet again."

Appendix

Dear Reader:

I feel honored to be able to share with you my story – a story of myself and my friends that ultimately interconnects with Bruce Lee's story and his legacy. The friendship that grew between Bruce, myself and our two friends left a mark upon all of us. It is something that is still evident in every facet of my life. There's not a day that goes by when I don't think of my friend, Bruce, and his impact.

In the summer of 2015, in front of 60,000 baseball fans, I watched Bruce's daughter Shannon walk across AT&T Park in San Francisco and listened to her perform the American National Anthem. We were all there to offer a tribute to my friend Bruce on what would have been his 75th birthday. In that moment I realized the players were no longer the San Francisco Giants or the New York Mets and the fans were no longer divided along team lines. Everyone in that stadium had become a part of one team: Bruce Lee's team. The players and audience alike were part of the millions and millions of Bruce Lee fans throughout the entire world who have been united by a single man and his vision. The same magnitude of Bruce Lee's power that had inspired me so many years ago inspired thousands at the stadium that day. It had been a long journey from a small Seattle garage where Bruce first started teaching, to the honor bestowed upon him by the major league baseball team in the city of his birth.

I found myself transported back to 1996 in Seattle where several of Bruce's first and second generation students got together to preserve his legacy. It was the beginning of an understanding that today has become the Bruce Lee Foundation. It makes me happy and proud to see that Shannon now carries on her father's legacy as the President of the Board of Directors of the Bruce Lee Foundation. I rest easy knowing that Bruce Lee's legacy will continue to inspire and help new generations for many years to come.

Like Bruce, the Foundation is always learning; always looking to ways to innovate itself and make a bigger impact in the world. Now in 2015, our organization is working on exciting new programs to not just keep Bruce's legacy alive, but to share his insights and empower people to be the best they can be and truly make a difference across the globe.

We are one big family – Bruce Lee's family. As his friend I invite you to visit www.bruceleefoundation.org and become part of his family too.

Until we meet again,

Allen Joe,
Member, Bruce Lee Foundation Board of Directors

Bibliography

"Bombing of Hiroshima and Nagasaki." *A&E Television Networks, LLC.* Accessed June 10, 2015. http://www.history.com/topics/world-war-ii/bombing-of-hiroshima-and-nagasaki.

Bruce Lee Foundation. Accessed March 24, 2015. http://www.bruceleefoundation.org/.

"Charles Atlas." *A&E Television Networks, LLC.* Accessed March 16, 2014. http://www.biography.com/people/charles-atlas-9191659.

"Chinese Immigration and the Chinese Exclusion Acts." *Office of the Historian, United States Department of State.* Accessed December 06, 2014. http://www.history.state.gov/milestones/1866-1898/chinese-immigration.

Gong, Tommy. *Bruce Lee. The Evolution of A Martial Artist.* Black Belt Books, a Division of Ohara Publications, Inc., 2014.

"Japanese Occupation of China Before World War II." *Jeffrey Hays.* Accessed July 04, 2015. http://www.factsanddetails.com/asian/ca67/sub426/item2537.html.

Joe, Allen and Brice Wong. "Interview With Allen Joe & SIFU Ted Wong's Martial Evolution." *Ted Wong Jeet Kune Do Magazine*, April 2012.

Little, John. *Bruce Lee. The Art of Expressing The Human Body.* Compiled and edited by John Little. Tuttle Publishing, 1998.

"President John F. Kennedy Speech on April 21st, 1961." Accessed January 20, 2015. http://www.62worldsfair.com/.

"Rosie the Riveter." *The Pop History Dig, LLC.* Accessed March 12, 2015. http://www.pophistorydig.com/topics/rosie-the-riveter-1941-1945/.

About the Authors

ALLEN JOE was the first Asian American to win the title of Mr. Northern California Bodybuilding Champion in 1946. He was one of Bruce Lee's closest friends and inspired Bruce to build up his body through proper training. Allen is a role model for the young martial artists demonstrating not only physical skills but also the values of friendship, respect and hard work. Allen has continued to love and support Bruce's family over the decades since Bruce passed away. At 92 years of age, Allen still lifts weights and stays in good shape.

After serving in World War II, Allen married his high school sweetheart Annie and they have been together for 69 years. Today, Allen serves on the Board of the Bruce Lee Foundation. He is esteemed as an Ambassador for the preservation of the legacy of his old friend Bruce.

DMITRI BOBKOV was born in Minsk, Belarus. He is the author of *Voice from the Past: Lies and Truth at the Bottom of the Biggest Criminal Case in Belarusian History*. Dmitri has been featured in Nasdaq Closing Bell Ceremony. He is a member of the National Press Club of Washington, D.C. Dmitri likes art and enjoys making sketches and portraits of his friends. He lives in the San Francisco Bay Area.

SVETLANA KIM is the author of *White Pearl and I: A Memoir of a Political Refugee*. She is also a speaker and radio talk show host. Svetlana was recognized with the Daily Point of Light Award by Points of Light established by the administration of President George H.B. Bush to honor individuals creating meaningful change in communities across America.

Svetlana was selected to be a spokesperson for the 2011 MACY'S Asian Pacific American Heritage Month. Kim has been featured and profiled in *The New Times, The Wall Street Journal, The Washington Post, MSN Money, MSNBC,* Nasdaq Closing Bell, and *The Gazette*, a publication of the Library of Congress. She is married and resides in the San Francisco Bay Area.

Visit the author's website at: svetlanakim.com

CPSIA information can be obtained at www.ICGtesting.com
Printed in the USA
LVOW11*0805291115
464520LV00010B/150/P